Live
Laugh
Laundry

Live
Laugh
Laundry

A calming guide to keeping your
clothes clean – and you happy

LAURA MOUNTFORD

EBURY
PRESS

Ebury Press an imprint of Ebury Publishing
20 Vauxhall Bridge Road
London SW1V 2SA

Ebury Press is part of the Penguin Random House group of companies
whose addresses can be found at global.penguinrandomhouse.com

Penguin
Random House
UK

First published by Ebury Press in 2023

www.penguin.co.uk

A CIP catalogue record for this book is available from the British Library

ISBN 9781529906561

Typeset in 10.75/18pt Futura LT Pro by Jouve (UK), Milton Keynes
Printed and bound in Great Britain by Clays Ltd, Elcograf S.p.A.

The authorised representative in the EEA is Penguin Random House Ireland,
Morrison Chambers, 32 Nassau Street, Dublin D02 YH68

Penguin Random House is committed to a sustainable
future for our business, our readers and our planet. This book
is made from Forest Stewardship Council® certified paper.

Contents

Hello, let's talk laundry!   1

Part 1: The laundry basics

1. Getting to know your washing machine   9
2. A guide to laundry products   23
3. Saving energy and money   39
4. Natural and eco-friendly laundry   51
5. Caring for your fabrics   63
6. The stain removal directory   83
7. Creating a laundry routine   103

Part 2: Next-level laundry

8. Laundry gadgets   113
9. Seasonal laundry tasks   123
10. Babies' and children's laundry   149
11. Laundry for your pets   157
12. Laundry on the go   167

Part 3: Not technically laundry (but still important!)

13. Drying   175
14. Ironing   187

A final note   203
The laundry products I can't live without   207
Thank you   213
About the author   215
Laundry notes   217

Hello, let's talk laundry!

Doing the laundry can feel like a never-ending story. No matter how many washes you put on, there *still* seems to be a huge pile in the basket. It often appears to be an endless task! So, this is why I have written this book – I want to make laundry not only easier for you, but also something that you *enjoy* doing.

With so many different products and washing symbols it's no wonder that most of us just throw things in the machine and hope for the best, but I will try to simplify everything and share my favourite tips and tricks so that no matter how much of a laundry lover you are right now, you can up your laundry game and make keeping your clothes fresh a breeze. I've written this book to be the perfect guide to keep in your laundry room, by your washing machine or on your bookshelf. You can grab this book whenever you need it, whether it be as a reminder of how to wash your winter coat or for an emergency tip on how to remove a stain from your clothes.

Live Laugh Laundry

When my younger brother and sister and I were teenagers living at home my mum, who was working full time as well as running a busy home, made us responsible for doing our own washing. My mum did not mess around when it came to doing her laundry. Every day she would wash, dry and iron with military precision (I have no doubt that my routine and consistency definitely come from her example). We each had our own basket, were shown what products to use, how to operate the machine and told that we could do our washing at any time of the day, as long as it wasn't in the evening when my mum did hers and my dad's. This was great delegation on her part, but it also set us all up for success when we eventually left the nest and moved into our own homes. (Although I remember on more than one occasion my brother James would put his clean washing back in his basket just so he didn't have to put it away!)

Fast-forward to when I was at university and spent some time studying in Canada. I had never lived away from my home in the UK, let alone in another country where I didn't know anyone or the area. I had a small room in student accommodation living with three other girls, two from Denmark and one from Romania. During this time, I realised that I loved my own company and home comforts. Although I really missed home, I eventually got into a routine and I found so much joy in doing basic tasks like cooking my dinner, tidying my room or going to the communal laundry room once a week to wash my bedding and clothes. I loved the feeling of having freshly washed bedding, towels and clothes; it made me feel like I was back at home.

Hello, let's talk laundry!

Now in my thirties and living with my partner Gavin and our two Italian greyhounds Luther and Enzo, the somewhat basic task of doing the laundry has helped me through some challenging times. Whether it be stressful periods at work or feeling not quite myself, I find doing the laundry very therapeutic. I think of it as an extension of my self-care routine. Like how I enjoy having a shower with my favourite body wash or having a pamper with skincare products, I love delving into my laundry cupboard and picking out products that will make my clothes, bedding and everything else smell divine and give them a pamper, too.

Having worked in retail for over 18 years, I also love clothes. I'm fascinated by different fabrics and styles, and I have so much fun styling and putting the perfect outfit together. Wearing an outfit that I am comfortable in makes me feel more confident and having fabrics that feel soft and smell fresh is another simple pleasure.

I also like to look after my things, a trait that I have definitely inherited from my dad who would wear his clothes until they were falling apart (if my mum would let him!). Looking after my clothes, making them last longer and being more conscious of how I treat them is something that is becoming more and more important to me as I get older. How we wash our clothes plays an important part in how long they last, and it's so important as it also helps us reduce the amount we send to landfill.

With the cost of living and energy prices increasing, this book will also provide some easy ways we can save money on our bills and reduce our impact on the environment at the same time, just by tweaking our laundry routines. I hope I can show you how making small changes can make a big difference.

So, my romanticising about the laundry might sound like I've lost the plot, but I believe that finding joy in the simple everyday things really has shifted my mindset and in some ways, especially on the tough days, it has been my saviour.

You might have come to this book to learn practical tips on how to make your laundry life easier (and you'll definitely get this!) but I hope it might also help you learn how to enjoy it as one of your self-care rituals, too. My laundry routine has helped me hugely on difficult days and I'd love for it to do the same for you.

We're all going on different journeys with our laundry, and it would be great to hear how you're getting on. Whether it be trying out something you have read in this book or you have a tip to share, I would love to hear from you so please use the hashtag #LiveLaughLaundry or tag me @lauracleanaholic on Instagram or TikTok.

Lots of love,

Laura x

PART 1

The *laundry* basics

1

Getting to know your washing machine

We bought our first washing machine a few years ago after making do with second-hand ones previously and it might sound silly but I felt really excited and lucky to have my own brand-new washing machine. I have a front-loading machine with the matching tumble dryer, and they sit next to each other in pride of place in my laundry room, which I feel very fortunate to have.

Whatever machine you have, getting to know your own washing machine will make your life so much easier. Don't worry if now you just put your clothes in the machine and hope for the best. This chapter will help you to make your washing machine work as efficiently as possible for you.

Buying a washing machine

There are so many different washing machines on the market, but fundamentally they all wash our clothes. My advice when buying a washing machine is that you don't need to spend a fortune. Try to get the best quality machine that you can for your money. Most likely, your washing machine will be one of the most used appliances in your home and if you can invest in a quality product, it should last longer and cost you less in breakdowns. So, doing your research is definitely worthwhile before you commit to a purchase as some brands can be unreliable.

The main factors to consider when purchasing a washing machine are the **drum capacity** you require for your household and the **energy efficiency rating**. We'll go into these two points in more detail below. Lots of models now have some fantastic additional features like smart technology – which allows you to remotely control your machine using your phone – noise reduction, and various programmes to make it as convenient as possible to select the correct temperature and spin speed you need for your wash. These additional features may or may not be important to you. But, if you love a gadget, then you'll almost certainly love one of these washing machines.

There are also combo washer dryers available that both wash and dry your clothes. I've found that while they are great for space saving, in my experience they are not particularly effective and are neither a good washing machine nor tumble dryer. As there are more functions, the likelihood of something going wrong with them also seems to be much higher. My preference then has always been to buy just a straightforward washing machine and have a separate tumble dryer.

Drum size

When choosing a new washing machine, it's important to consider the drum size that is suitable for your household and lifestyle. A machine with a larger capacity may use more energy to run, but if you have a larger drum size, this could actually *save* you energy because you can wash more in one load, therefore reducing the amount of times you have to use your machine each week. Our washing machine has a 9kg capacity which is relatively high considering there are only two of us plus the dogs in our household. However, we chose a high-capacity machine because it means we can wash more in every load we do rather than do multiple loads every day. Regardless of the size of your washing machine drum, aim to reduce the amount of washing loads you do each week by waiting until you have a full load to wash. Even if you only reduced the number of washes you do by one each week, that would be a total of 52 fewer wash loads over a year.

Overloading and cramming too many items into your machine, however, will mean that your clothes won't be washed effectively as there isn't enough space for the water and detergent to clean them. It could also damage your machine as the drum will be unbalanced. A larger drum will mean your machine is slightly deeper, so you shouldn't require any additional space in terms of height and width, your machine might just stick out a little more.

If you don't quite know where to start on which size would be best for your household, here are some rough guidelines:

12kg+ Extra large
This is ideal for a large, active family.

8–9kg Large
This size is great for a small family and for washing a full set of bedding all in one go.

7kg Standard
This is ideal for a couple or if you are an active person who lives on your own.

6kg Small
This is great for one person.

Energy efficiency
When looking to buy a new washing machine, you also want to aim to purchase one that has a high energy rating as this means that it will be more energy efficient and reduce your energy

consumption. Appliances are given an energy rating on a scale of A to G with A being the most efficient product of its class and G being the least efficient.

Many modern washing machines have useful energy-saving and eco-mode functions, and some even have automatic dosing systems so that the machine is only using the amount of detergent and fabric conditioner required for the wash to help you reduce any product wastage.

When using eco functions the washes tend to take longer. You may question how, if the wash is taking longer, it could be saving energy? The answer is that when in eco-mode the cycle is slower because the water takes longer to heat up and is kept at a lower temperature, which uses less energy. Think of it as walking versus driving to work: both options will get you to work and while walking will take longer, it has no impact on the environment. In comparison, driving is quicker but it will cost you more in fuel and have a negative impact on the environment.

Laundry settings

Now that you know more about the two fundamentals of understanding your perfect machine, it's time to delve into the possible laundry settings that the machine offers. There are so many different functions and settings that it can make doing the laundry quite mind-boggling for many of us. However, hopefully this section will help to make navigating your washing machine as simple as possible for you.

The two most important things to know about your machine settings are the **spin speed** of the wash and the **temperature** of the wash. The various different functions that you see around the main dial or on the menu screen are simply programmed to make it as convenient as possible for you, with the spin speed and temperature already selected. For example, a delicate wash setting would have a low temperature and a low spin speed, while a cotton wash would have a high temperature and a fast spin speed. Here are some of the main settings you might find:

Cottons

This is best for bedding and towels as it has a higher spin speed suitable for these fabrics but is too harsh for some clothes.

Synthetics

This is ideal for gym gear or other clothes made from synthetic fabrics as it has a low spin speed.

Delicates

This is best for washing blouses and lingerie as it is a cycle with a low spin speed.

Quick wash

This is really handy for wash loads with light soiling, but it should not be used for delicates. It has a high spin speed and is usually finished within half an hour.

Hand wash

This can be used for items even when the care label states 'hand wash only' and is useful for very delicate clothing. This cycle has a low spin speed to prevent any ripping and stretching.

There will most likely also be options to add a **pre-wash** or a **rinse/spin**. A pre-wash is great for particularly dirty or stained clothes because it gives an extra starter wash and then drains the dirty water before the main wash. An extra rinse is ideal for making sure that all of the detergent has been removed from the fabric. It is also worth adding an extra rinse if you have put stain remover in the wash for your children's clothes to make sure there is no residue left, which might irritate their skin. It is also useful for heavily soiled clothes, for fabrics like towels and bed sheets or if you have very sensitive skin to ensure that there are no suds or product residue left behind when the cycle finishes. An extra spin is really great for removing as much moisture as possible from the wash too, which then reduces drying time.

You may wish to look in your handbook so that you are familiar with each of the settings for your machine. However, if all the settings feel quite overwhelming, I have to admit that for the vast majority of my washes I tend to use a cool wash of 40°C or lower and a fast spin speed, which seems to have served me well over the years. My only exceptions would be delicate fabrics, like wool, and items that are particularly dirty or have stains. If you're not a laundry fanatic, don't get bogged down with all of the different settings on your washing machine. In reality, you really only need to use a couple of them for your day-to-day laundry.

The drawer

So, we've covered the types of machine and the most important settings. Now, it's time to tackle the drawer as it's critical you know what product should go where.

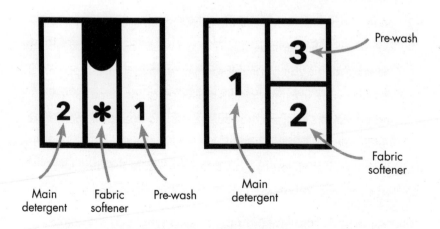

Getting to know your washing machine

There are normally three sections in the washing machine drawer that will release whatever product you put in it during different stages of the cycle. If you're unfamiliar with some of the products I mention below, don't worry, we'll go into this more in chapter 2.

1. **Pre-wash** A pre-wash is used to soak items that are particularly smelly, soiled or stained. It is an extra wash at the beginning of the cycle and the filthy water is drained out before the main wash begins. This section of the drawer is for detergent that will be used for the pre-wash. You can just use the same detergent as the main wash for extra freshness or, alternatively, a stain remover providing it is not bleach. (Using bleach in the pre-wash will reduce the effectiveness of the detergent in the main wash as it destroys the enzymes and any whiteners.) You only need a tablespoon of detergent for a pre-wash.

2. **Main wash** This section of the drawer is for your main detergent, whether it be liquid or powder. You can also add oxi powder to this compartment to help remove stains. I recommend reading your washing machine user guide as some manufacturers suggest that detergents should be diluted before being used in their machines. Usually detergents come with a lid or scoop so that you can accurately measure the amount of product required depending on how big the wash load is.

3. **Conditioner** This section of the drawer is for fabric conditioner/softener. Whatever is poured into this section will be released into the machine towards the end of the wash before

the spin. If you are using a laundry cleanser or sanitiser, this should also be poured into this section of the drawer.

LAURA'S LITTLE LAUNDRY TIPS

You can add a cup of white vinegar to the fabric softener section of your washing machine drawer, which is a great natural deodoriser and leaves your towels lovely and fluffy. It is also best to switch fabric conditioner for white vinegar when washing your microfibre cleaning cloths as softener can reduce their absorbency over time.

How to clean your washing machine

My most popular videos on social media are the ones showing how I clean my washing machine. It is one of those things that nobody ever teaches you how to do and it is funny to think that me cleaning my washing machine has been watched by millions of people around the world!

To help you to get the most out of your washing machine, it is important that you maintain and look after your machine to prolong its life and ensure that it continues to work effectively cleaning your clothes for as long as possible. After all, nobody wants to have to pay for a breakdown or the inconvenience of having a washing machine that does not work!

Getting to know your washing machine

Cleaning your washing machine removes any build-up of detergent and softener or stagnant water, which could cause your appliance to smell. It improves the results of the wash, reducing the likelihood of any spots or marks caused by the machine, and it also ensures that the inside of the machine is hygienically clean by removing any lingering germs.

I aim to clean my washing machine every month to keep it smelling fresh and kill any bacteria. We live in the south of the UK which is a particularly hard water area so limescale is a nightmare as it builds up quickly on appliances. Cleaning your washing machine monthly might feel like too often for you and your schedule, but try to fit it in when you can as it'll help ensure your laundry is as clean as it can be and save stress later down the line.

There are lots of products on the market that make cleaning your washing machine really convenient, but showing your washing machine some TLC doesn't have to break the bank. You can do it cheaply and effectively using this method:

Step 1 – Remove the drawer, clean it in a bowl of hot soapy water and rinse thoroughly. If you don't want to wash the whole machine, or don't have time to, you can just do this step. You should do this regularly to keep it smelling fresh and to avoid any blockages.

Step 2 – Clean behind the drawer by spraying a bathroom cleaner or white vinegar to remove any mould and limescale. Leave for a few minutes so that the product can work its magic and wipe thoroughly with a cloth.

Step 3 – Next, clean and empty the filter. This is usually behind a small door on the front at the bottom of the machine. You can drain the filter using the small hose that is attached or unscrew it but be careful as the water will drain out quickly so lay down an oven tray and a tea towel or absorbent cloth to soak it up (one of my followers on TikTok suggested using a nappy!). You may also find the odd penny or hairclip that went astray in the wash!

Step 4 – Clean the rubber seal around the door, getting stuck in there and removing any debris. A bathroom cleaner or white vinegar works well for this but be sure not to use any products containing bleach as this can damage the rubber.

Step 5 – Finally, clean the drum. I pour a packet of soda crystals into the drum, a cup of white vinegar or disinfectant into the drawer and then put the empty machine on a hot wash cycle. My washing machine has a drum clean setting and this is equivalent to a 90°C cotton cycle and usually lasts for about an hour.

LAURA'S LITTLE LAUNDRY TIPS

Keep your washing machine smelling fresh and reduce the growth of mould or bacteria by leaving the door and drawer open when it is not in use.

Getting to know your washing machine

Look after your washing machine and it will make your laundry life so much easier! Get to know your own appliance and don't worry about all the different functions; find out which ones work best for you. Clean your machine regularly to avoid a build-up of mould or limescale and it should continue to operate effectively for years to come. Think of it as self-care for you *and* your washing machine. By investing a little time in giving it some love and attention every now and then, in return it will cause you much less stress and make your life easier, too.

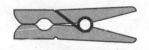

"You know what I figure?
If I can do laundry,
there's nothing
I can't do."

Rachel Green in Friends

2

A guide to laundry products

Some girls have loads of shoes and handbags . . . I have loads of laundry products! I love trying new products and fragrances and I really enjoy sharing my favourites on social media – it seems that so many of you have a passion for laundry products too! I guess my laundry products are the equivalent of having lots of different beauty products or make-up. If they make you feel good and bring you joy as well as making an everyday task like doing the laundry more exciting, then surely that's not a bad thing? In fact, it's trying the different products and finding my favourites that actually motivates me to get my laundry done!

We are spoilt for choice now with so many different laundry products to try but it can be a little overwhelming unless you know exactly what each category is for. This section is a guide to the main laundry products and what they are used for along with a few of my top tips to help you choose the right products for you.

Laundry detergents

The most important laundry product is the detergent that you use to actually wash your clothes and get rid of the dirt. They come in so many different forms now so it can be quite confusing but essentially they all do the same thing which is clean your clothes. The most widely used are liquids, powders, gels and capsules, all with different benefits.

Liquid and gel detergents

Liquid detergents and gels are good all-rounders as they dissolve easily in the machine and are suitable for cool and quick washes. You can also use them to pre-treat stains by applying them directly to fabrics. They are usually good value for money but often more expensive than powder.

Powdered detergents

Powdered detergents are a more traditional product – they are usually the best value for money but can be bulky so transporting the boxes and storing them is not as convenient. Powders can be added directly to the drum or in the drawer but they need to dissolve properly before they start to work so are not always effective in cooler washes.

Laundry capsules

Capsules are a popular choice as they are convenient because the dosage is pre-measured and there is no mess. Capsules should be added directly to the empty drum before adding your dirty laundry so that they dissolve correctly and do not stick in the rubber seal.

Detergents are either biological (bio) or non-biological (non-bio) and the difference between the two is that non-bio products do not contain enzymes. Here is a little bit more information to help understand the differences between them:

Bio

Bio laundry detergents contain enzymes that help to break down dirt and stains. They are best used for cool washes as anything that is too hot can break down these enzymes and cause them not to be as effective against stains. You can usually spot a biological product as the packaging or lid tends to be green. If it does not state that the product is non-biological, then the chances are that it will be a bio product.

Non-bio

Non-bio laundry detergents do not contain enzymes, meaning they are more gentle so can be more suitable if you have sensitive skin. Although they do not contain enzymes, modern non-bio detergents can still be really effective at cleaning fabrics and keeping them fresh, but to remove stubborn stains you may need to use a slightly hotter wash for them to be most effective. You can usually tell whether a detergent is non-bio as the packaging tends to be blue.

Detergent for delicates

There are many laundry detergents that are specially formulated for washing delicates like wool and silk. These products are mild and do not contain enzymes, brighteners or bleaching agents that can shrink or damage your delicate fabrics.

Strong, mild or gentle?

Knowing whether to use bio, non-bio or a delicate detergent can be confusing, but the simplest way to think about it is to use non-bio for babies and if anyone in your family has sensitive skin, a delicate detergent for fabrics like wool and silk and a bio detergent for everything else. The good news is that they can all be used in the same way to wash your clothes in the machine.

How much detergent to use?

You should always follow the instructions on the packaging of whatever laundry detergent you choose to use; most have a measuring cap to make it as easy as possible. Do not be tempted to use too much product as although you might think that it will make your fabrics fresher, it actually has the opposite effect. If you use too much product, it may not dissolve properly in the wash, leaving residue on your clothes which will eventually cause them to crisp and even smell musty.

When measuring the correct dosage consider how dirty the items are and how big the load is. If you live in a hard water area, you may need to use more detergent as the natural minerals in the water will prevent the detergent from soaping up as easily.

Fabric conditioner

Fabric conditioner, or softener as it is often called, is a liquid that you can add to your wash to give softness along with extra freshness and scent. It also helps to reduce wrinkling by smoothing and flattening fibres, protects fabrics from stretching, bobbling and fading and can speed up drying time too.

You pour fabric conditioner into the dispenser drawer usually marked with a flower symbol and during the last rinse cycle water will flow into the compartment and transfer it into the drum, mixing it with your laundry. You should not put fabric conditioner directly into the drum as it works only in the last rinse cycle.

When washing fabrics they can become rough when dried so adding a quality fabric softener reduces the friction between the fibres, detangling them and protecting them so that when they are dry they feel softer against our skin. Fabric conditioners are now available in so many different gorgeous scents, I like to think of them as perfume for my clothes. I love doing the 'sniff test' and trying different fragrances.

Fabric conditioners are not suitable for certain fabrics like fluffy fleece, terry cloth, microfibres, sportswear or flame-resistant garments as they can break down their flame resistance and absorbency. To keep these smelling fresh you can use either white vinegar to neutralise any odours or in-wash scent boosters.

Scent boosters

Scent boosters are little beads that can be added to the drum of your machine to give an even longer-lasting freshness and fragrance to your fabrics. The beads dissolve in the wash and the perfume is infused into your clothes. Something I like to do is to match my laundry detergent, fabric conditioner and scent boosters to give my clothes an extra scent boost that lasts for ages. Even when I've washed and dried my clothes or bedding and stored them away they still stay smelling lovely and fresh for ages rather than going musty.

LAURA'S LITTLE LAUNDRY TIPS

The great thing about scent boosters is that they smell so divine I love to use them not just in my washing machine but also all around my home. I buy the little mesh organza bags online, fill them with scent boosters and use them in my wardrobe, cupboards, in my bins to keep them fresh, in my vases with artificial flowers and even in my car.

Laundry cleansers

Laundry cleansers are designed to kill bacteria and viruses in the wash. You use a laundry cleanser with your choice of detergent but you pour it into the fabric conditioner section of the drawer. A laundry cleanser is ideal if you have a sickness bug in your household but also when you wash on cooler temperatures below

60°C because bacteria can still survive in your washing machine when using detergent alone at this temperature. A laundry cleanser then helps to keep your fabrics hygienic while avoiding using hot wash cycles, saving energy and money. Laundry cleansers also kill odour-causing bacteria on your fabrics and leave them smelling fresh.

I like to use laundry cleansers to wash my cleaning cloths to keep them smelling fresh and to ensure that they are as hygienic as possible. Cleaning cloths should not be washed with fabric conditioner as it can damage the fibres and their absorbency so switch to a laundry cleanser as a great way to ensure they are not only hygienic but also smell lovely and fresh.

I don't tend to use a laundry cleanser for other washes as it is simply not necessary, but they are great for adding to every wash if one of us has a sickness bug as it helps to stop it spreading.

Oxi stain-remover products

Oxi powders and sprays are used to remove stubborn stains. Unlike bleach, they do not contain chlorine so they are safer to use on your fabrics. Instead, oxi products release active oxygen to lift stains and odours easily out of fabrics even on low washing temperatures. Oxi sprays can be used to pre-treat items before you put them in the wash. Alternatively, oxi powders can be used for pre-treating by mixing into a paste or putting into the wash either directly in the drum or in the drawer along with your detergent.

There are now lots of oxi products available to buy whether you need them to remove stains and keep your whites bright or to protect your colours, so you can select the correct type of product depending on the item you need to remove a stain from.

Bleach

Chlorine bleach is commonly used for laundry as it has both sanitising and whitening properties, converting stains into colourless, soluble particles that can be easily washed away with water. However, it is a particularly toxic corrosive product and should be used with caution as it can ruin fabrics, leaving faded patches and even burning them in some cases. I don't tend to use bleach in my laundry as I have not found it necessary and there are many other products that can effectively remove stains and brighten whites without the need for it.

LAURA'S LITTLE LAUNDRY TIPS

Don't throw away dirty dull white socks, try refreshing them by pre-treating using an oxi stain-remover spray. Leave for the time recommended on the product packaging and then wash in your machine using an oxi powder. You will be amazed at how their brightness is restored.

Colour catchers/collectors

Colour catchers or collectors are sheets or cloths that you add to your wash to protect your laundry and prevent colour dye running, dulling garments. Over time washing different colours together will eventually cause a layer of mixed colours to ruin your fabrics so colour catchers allow mixed washes as they act as a magnet, trapping any loose dye from the water. Using colour catchers also prevents garments going grey or losing their brightness. When you finish the wash you can see all of the dye trapped in the sheet that otherwise would have been mixed in the wash. Colour catchers are really useful as they save you time, energy and water as you don't have to sort different colours into different washes. You can even mix your whites and colours using a colour catcher but I don't tend to do this as I prefer to use a whitening oxi powder in with a separate white wash to keep my whites lovely and bright.

Tumble dryer sheets

Tumble dryer sheets can be used to preserve freshness and add fragrance when using your tumble dryer. They also reduce creasing and static. I try not to use our tumble dryer too frequently and dry naturally whenever possible to save energy and money as it can be quite expensive. However, I do use it for bedding and towels and using a tumble dryer sheet means that they stay fresher and I don't have to iron the bedding! Living in the UK, it can be quite wet and miserable, particularly in the autumn and winter months, so having a tumble dryer is handy, especially as I live in an old barn that can get damp with lots of washing hanging indoors.

LAURA'S LITTLE LAUNDRY TIPS
The thing I absolutely love about tumble dryer sheets is that because they smell so amazing I also use them to keep other items fresh. Pop them in your drawers to keep your clothes fresh, in your suitcase when you travel, under the seat in your car and even in your shoes and slippers!

Crease releasers

Crease releasers are a relatively new product that you spritz on fabrics once they are washed and dried to remove creases without having to use the iron. If you're anything like me and hate ironing, then a crease releaser is a really handy product to have, especially for items that are bulky or difficult to iron, and they are also useful for packing in your bag when you are on the go or travelling. We love to go away with the dogs in our campervan so a crease releaser is really handy to pack as if I rarely iron at home, there's certainly no way I will be ironing on holiday! I love the scents of some of the crease releasers available. They really are like a perfume for your fabrics, freshening them up and relaxing the fibres to remove wrinkles at the same time. I love using a crease releaser when ironing bedding as it helps to make it easier and smells incredible too. Be careful when using crease releasers as they can make surfaces slippery due to their fibre-relaxing formula so always pop a towel down to protect the floor when spritzing.

Ironing water

Ironing water, or de-ionised water, will stop a build-up of limescale in your iron and also make ironing easier, helping to remove stubborn creases with a fresh scent. Be sure to read the packaging as some of the perfumed ironing water is not suitable for steam generator irons.

Laura's little self-care tips

I am obsessed with matching my laundry products; I love having the whole collection of products in the same scent and using them for a wash as part of my laundry routine, in the same way that for fragrances I love I buy everything in that scent. My favourites are The White Company, Jo Malone and Neom scents and I have everything from the shower gel and handwash to the candles and reed diffusers. If they made laundry products, I would definitely buy them too! We are spoilt for choice now with scent combinations for our laundry that smell absolutely divine and even though I love trying them all out, I still keep coming back to Lenor's Exotic Bloom.

> It's such a gorgeous scent; mysterious yet cosy at the same time with both fruity and floral notes. I have the laundry pods, fabric softener and in-wash scent boosters in this scent. I also love Fairy as it is such a classic nostalgic scent and reminds me of home and growing up.

There really are so many different laundry products readily available to buy now, and hopefully after reading this chapter you will find it easier to navigate the laundry aisle next time you are shopping. I find that treating myself to a new laundry product gives me a boost of motivation – whether that's trying a new scent combination or testing a new product that I have not used before. I find it is a simple pleasure to turn what would otherwise be a very boring job into something I enjoy. I guess you could say it's like trying out a new recipe for someone who likes to cook (I'm terrible at cooking by the way) or buying new workout gear to motivate you to go to the gym. It is also so satisfying to see the before and after photos when removing a stain so even if you don't post on Instagram like I do, it is worthwhile doing so you can see what a difference your efforts have made.

Laundry essentials shopping checklist:

- ☐ Bio detergent (powder, liquid, gel or capsules)
- ☐ Non-bio detergent (powder, liquid, gel or capsules)
- ☐ Detergent for delicates
- ☐ White vinegar
- ☐ Soda crystals (see page 53)
- ☐ Fabric softener
- ☐ Scent boosters
- ☐ Colour collector sheets
- ☐ Mesh laundry bags (see page 115)
- ☐ Tumble dryer sheets
- ☐ Oxi powder for whites
- ☐ Oxi powder for colours
- ☐ Oxi stain-remover spray
- ☐ Crease releaser
- ☐ Ironing water

Laura's little self-care tips

Organise your space. Whether you have a small shelf next to your washing machine or a dream laundry room, organise your space to make it easy to grab the products you need. Think about where you store your laundry products. Aim for the cupboard or shelf to be as easy as possible to access near your washing machine. Keep the cupboard as neat and tidy as possible so you don't have to waste time delving to the back of a messy cupboard to search for the product you need. If buying in bulk, then store any excess somewhere else like the garage or cupboard under the stairs so that you can just restock when you need to.

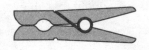

This home has endless
love and laundry.

3

Saving energy and money

With the ever-rising costs of living and our increased concerns about our impact on the environment, many of us are seeking savvy ways to reduce both our spending and our carbon footprint.

I believe that small changes really can make a big difference and as doing the laundry is a frequent task in every household, there are many little switches to our routines that, if more of us made them, would have a big impact on the environment. I think that while many of us would agree that we want to make more environmentally conscious decisions, it can be tough – we lead busy lives and so naturally favour convenience. However, hopefully these easy changes will help to highlight some of the small things that we could all try to implement in our households to not only reduce the impact that doing our laundry has on the environment but also to help us save money too.

How to save energy

There are some super simple changes that you can make to help reduce energy consumption when using your washing machine.

Wash less often

The simplest way to reduce energy usage is to wash less frequently and only wash clothes when they actually need it (i.e. when they are dirty and smelly). I must admit, I used to wash everything after just one wear which seems silly to me now, especially if it had only been worn for a few hours and wasn't even dirty! Most items just need hanging and airing for a freshen up and can then be re-worn – they only really need washing after a few wears. This will not only save you money on your energy bills and reduce the amount of laundry product you use but it will also help to prolong the life of the clothes in your wardrobe.

Wash on a cool temperature

The other simple way to save energy is to reduce the temperature of your wash cycles. The majority of electricity used in your washing machine cycle is to heat up the water and for most washes this is unnecessary. Many detergents will effectively wash everyday fabrics at temperatures as low as 20°C, which when you stop to think about it isn't really a 'cold' temperature at all. Check the packaging to see if your chosen detergent is suitable for cool washes as most tend to make it clear as a benefit to using their product. In reality, most laundry loads are done to simply freshen up fabrics and do not require a hot wash so, unless you have a particularly soiled wash load or a sickness bug in your family, then there really is no need to crank up the temperature. If you have mucky PE kits to contend with or children who never seem to be able to eat without ending up wearing half of their dinner, then don't worry, you too can wash at a lower temperature – simply give the items a spritz with a stain remover first or add oxi powder to the wash.

Biological detergents usually work more efficiently at lower temperatures as the cleaning enzymes they contain can be less effective at removing stains in hotter water. Another way to help you to reduce the temperature of your laundry load and still kill bacteria and bugs is to use a laundry cleanser.

Check the dosage
It is also important to use the correct dosage of product when putting a wash load on as overusing can cause excess bubbles which, although they may look very satisfying, will take longer to rinse through and can leave a residue of product on your fabrics, causing them to feel stiff and smell musty over time.

Switch it off
Another simple thing that you can do is ensure that you switch off your machine rather than leaving it on standby mode. Ideally, if

you can turn your machine off at the mains and unplug it, then that will save the most energy, but if like me your socket is behind the machine and not easily accessible, then as long as no lights are on the display it should indicate that it is not on standby mode.

Thoughtful drying

How we dry our laundry also has an impact on cost and energy consumption. I must admit, in the damp winters here in the UK I am guilty of regularly using my tumble dryer; however, I am now more conscious about when I choose to use it and often dry either outdoors or on an airer indoors. Using the tumble dryer is expensive and thirsty when it comes to using energy so being more mindful about when I use it really has made a difference. Invest in a quality airer for indoors and a washing line for outdoors. You would be surprised that even on a cloudy day your laundry will still dry outdoors eventually. Adding an extra spin to your wash cycle is also a really easy way to help reduce the drying time of your laundry load as it's more energy efficient than a tumble dryer.

Reducing your carbon footprint

The products we choose to use for our laundry not only have an impact on how much we spend but also on our carbon footprint. There are so many factors to consider, including how the product is tested and manufactured, the ingredients used, how much water is included in the product and the delivery carbon footprint.

It is fantastic to see that many manufacturers of laundry products are considering their impact on the environment and making significant changes that make our buying decisions not only more sustainable but also cost effective. Recycled and plastic-free packaging are all slowly becoming standard and this is a huge step change. You can visit the websites of your favourite laundry brands to find out what they are doing to commit to making a change. Many elements of the manufacturing and distribution process are being improved by brands to reduce their impact on the environment.

Choose concentrated

Many laundry products are now available in concentrated formulas which have a number of benefits as they require less packaging and reduced transportation costs which is a significant contributing factor to the carbon footprint of a product.

Be a savvy shopper

To save money I tend to stock up when my favourite products are on special offer or buy larger-sized packs which are generally better value for money. The best way to work out if a product is good value for money or not when it is on special offer is to calculate the cost per wash. Most shelf-edge tickets in supermarkets will have already done this for you but if not, then it is simply the cost of the product divided by the number of washes you will get from the pack. Laundry packaging usually states how many washes the product should give you. I love getting a bargain and hate being ripped off so find that this has helped me know I am getting a good deal. When buying bigger value packs this also reduces the frequency that you will have to restock so saving you time and money.

LAURA'S LITTLE LAUNDRY TIPS

To ensure you get the best value for money when purchasing your laundry products, work out the cost per wash:

Cost of product divided by the number of washes

e.g. A product costing £2.99 that says it does 28 washes will be 10.7p per wash

When you think about it there are so many ways that we can all tweak our laundry routines to save money and also reduce our energy consumption and impact on the environment at the same time. If we all made some small changes to our laundry habits, then it really would make a big difference.

How much your washing machine costs to run

If you search for the make and model number of your washing machine, then you can find the product information for it. This is

Savvy laundry checklist:

- ❏ Aim to reduce the amount of wash loads you put on per week and try to fill your machine each time you use it.

- ❏ Only wash items that are dirty, not just after one use.

- ❏ Switch to washing at cooler temperatures wherever possible; as low as 20°C is sufficient to freshen up most wash loads.

- ❏ Choose an energy-efficient washing machine.

- ❏ If your machine has an eco function, then switch to using that.

- ❏ Use a laundry cleanser to kill bacteria and viruses in the wash rather than using the highest temperatures.

- ❏ Do not overuse detergent or fabric conditioner.

- ❏ Dry your laundry naturally whenever possible. Add an extra spin to the end of the wash to speed up the drying process.

- ❏ Buy laundry products when they are on special offer or bigger value pack sizes. Calculate the cost per wash to ensure you are getting the best deal.

- ❏ Choose products with packaging that is plastic-free or made from recycled plastic.

- ❏ Clean your washing machine regularly so that it continues to work effectively and efficiently.

such a useful activity for figuring out just how much energy and water you could be saving when doing your laundry.

Look for the energy consumption in kwh (kilowatt hours), and then multiply it by the price per unit of energy. This is listed in the user guide for your appliance.*

My machine has a 9kg drum capacity which is equivalent to roughly 45 shirts per wash (you can find this information out for your washing machine online) and the data is based on a full wash load. Now, as much as I have lots of clothes, I don't think I have ever had 45 shirts to wash all at the same time! When I figured this out, it made me realise I should be filling up my washing machine far more than I am, and not just washing when I only have a few items.

In case it's useful, I also figured out the cost difference between using the different temperature settings on my washing machine, to highlight how much it's possible to save over the year by just switching to cooler washes and reducing the number of washes you put on each week.†

---

* For the calculation below, I've used 34p as my price per unit of energy as, at the time of writing, the price cap in the UK is going up significantly, so I want to calculate the cost of electricity for our various appliances.

† It's worth noting that the energy rating of my washing machine is A+++, which is particularly efficient, and this is one of the reasons we purchased this particular machine. Your washing machine may be different, depending on both its efficiency rating and drum size.

Saving energy and money

Hot 60°C cotton wash
0.92 kwh (full load) x 34p per kwh = 31p per wash
*365 washes per year = **£113.15 per year***
*208 washes per year (four times per week) = **£64.48 per year***
*156 washes per year (three times per week) = **£48.36 per year***

Cooler 40°C cotton wash
0.6 kwh (full load) x 34p per kwh = 20p per wash
*365 washes per year = **£73 per year***
*208 washes per year (four times per week) = **£41.60 per year***
*156 washes per year (three times per week) = **£31.20 per year***

So, even if I used my washing machine every single day, I would still save **£40.15** per year just by switching from a hot wash to a cooler wash. I now wash at even lower temperatures (30°C and 20°C) as for most loads, unless fabrics are heavily soiled, this is sufficient so I will be saving even more. You can also see from the calculations that by reducing the amount of wash loads you put on per week you can save both more money and energy at the same time.

We also tend to forget just how much water our washing machines use and how, by reducing the amount of wash loads we do per week, we can significantly minimise this. My washing machine uses 11,220 litres of water per year, based on 220 washes, so this is 51 litres of water per wash. That's just over four washes per week but say I reduced this to three washes per week, then I would be saving a huge 2,652 litres of water per year! Have a look at the water consumption for your washing machine by looking at the manual online. I was really surprised as I had never looked into it before but it has certainly prickled my conscience and made me think more about the small changes I can make to reduce my impact on the environment.

How much your tumble dryer costs to run

My tumble dryer is a condenser tumble dryer which has a B energy rating. Using the same method as above for my washing machine, this is how much it costs me (accurate at the time of writing) to run each load.

Full load 4.61kwh x 34p per kwh = £1.57 per cycle
*365 loads per year = **£573.05 per year***
*208 loads per year (four times per week) = **£326.56 per year***
*156 loads per year (three times per week) = **£244.92 per year***
*52 loads per year (once a week) = **£81.64 per year***

Half load 2.59 kwh x 34p per kwh = £0.88 per cycle
*365 loads per year = **£321.20 per year***
*208 loads per year (four times per week) = **£183.04 per year***
*156 loads per year (three times per week) = **£137.28 per year***
*52 loads per year (once a week) = **£45.76 per year***

As you can see from the calculations above, a tumble dryer is *very* hungry when it comes to eating up electricity! It makes me question how much I use it and how I can really easily save money and energy by only using it when *absolutely* necessary. If you have a tumble dryer and are looking to save money, it's worth being selective with when you choose your dryer over air drying.

Laura's little self-care tips
Review the cost of your washing machine and tumble dryer and set yourself a saving challenge. You could aim to use the money you save for a self-care treat for yourself, perhaps a new candle, a manicure, a takeaway or whatever you fancy.

Hopefully this section has inspired you to think about the switches that you could make to do your bit. I am far from perfect and sometimes it is easy to feel guilty and overwhelmed that you are not doing enough, but, in reality, it is better to do something rather than nothing at all. We need to be kinder to ourselves and our planet, so taking conscious steps that are also achievable within our daily routines really can make a difference.

I'd love to know what changes you have made and also for you to share any other money- and energy-saving laundry tips that you have to help inspire others at #LiveLaughLaundry and tag me @lauracleanaholic.

It all comes out
in the wash.

4

Natural and eco-friendly laundry

If you're being more cautious about how your laundry routine affects the planet, there's lots of options for products that can make your laundry much more environmentally friendly.

Traditional products like white vinegar and soda crystals are starting to come back into favour as natural alternatives. As the demand for more environmentally friendly products increases, more eco-friendly solutions are also slowly becoming more readily available. The challenge in order for these products to gain in popularity is for them to be sustainable but still deliver the same clean, fresh results we expect at a price that is affordable for more households.

There are many natural, traditional products that are versatile for your laundry and deliver great results. They are also inexpensive, and you can use them for lots of other cleaning tasks around your home. Our parents and grandparents would have used these for generations but, as more of a variety of products became readily available, they started to be overlooked (unfairly in my opinion!). So, next time you run out of one of your laundry products, consider some of these alternatives.

Laundry bars

An old-fashioned, traditional product that was used for centuries before washing machines revolutionised our laundry routines. Laundry bars can be used dry by directly rubbing onto fabrics to treat stains before putting the item in the machine. They can also be used to hand wash delicates with warm water like a bar of soap. You can even grate the laundry bar using a cheese grater and add directly into the machine. Be sure to check the correct dosage for your machine and the load size. You can grate the whole bar and store in an airtight jar so you don't need to crack out the cheese grater every time you want to pop a wash on! You can also use the shavings to make your own liquid laundry soap by heating it and letting it dissolve.

White vinegar

Distilled white vinegar is a fantastic natural laundry product and a must-have for every household as it is so versatile and inexpensive, not just as a laundry aid, but for cleaning too. It can be used to reduce odours, whiten and brighten fabrics, remove deodorant stains, soften fabrics and reduce lint and pet hair. Simply add a cupful to the fabric conditioner section of your washer drawer before putting on the wash.

LAURA'S LITTLE LAUNDRY TIPS

Remove underarm sweat and deodorant stains from garments by spraying generously with distilled white vinegar. Allow the vinegar to work for at least 10 minutes before washing the garment as normal in your washing machine.

Soda crystals

Soda crystals are a traditional natural laundry product and because of this they are often referred to as washing soda. My mum always has them in her cupboard along with a little scoop and now I do too as they are very inexpensive and are great for a multitude of uses around your home.

Soda crystals can be used to boost your laundry detergent, helping to remove stains and soften the water, saving you money as you will need less detergent if you live in a hard water area. Simply add a tablespoon to your detergent with every wash.

To remove stubborn stains from items, make up a strong solution (100g soda crystals in 500ml hot water) and soak for one hour before washing. I also use soda crystals to clean my washing machine as mentioned in chapter 1. By using them regularly it will help keep your washing machine free of limescale and detergent build-up.

LAURA'S LITTLE LAUNDRY TIPS

If your towels are feeling a little stiff and crunchy, then it's most likely that they have a build-up of product and limescale residue. To restore towels to their fluffy texture, try soaking them in a mixture of soda crystals and warm water. Leave to soak overnight, rinse thoroughly and then wash them as normal with half a cup of white vinegar in the fabric conditioner drawer.

Eco-friendly detergents and fabric conditioners are free from harsh chemicals and potentially harmful ingredients, usually with only natural colours and fragrances. There are also products that are cruelty-free, plant-based, biodegradable and those in recyclable packaging or made from recycled materials.

There are some innovative eco-friendly solutions now available to buy. Here are a few of the main eco-friendly products.

Laundry Ecoegg

You fill the Ecoegg with pellets and it can be reused multiple times in your machine before being refilled. It is designed to replace your detergent and fabric softener. The Ecoegg and pellets received a *Good Housekeeping* Getting Greener Award for reducing plastic.

Laundry sheets

Laundry sheets are pre-cut, pre-measured, concentrated sheets of laundry detergent without liquid or plastic packaging. They contain natural ingredients to clean our clothes in a sheet that dissolves in your wash made from biodegradable paper. These can be used to replace detergents in another form and are also popular for doing your laundry while travelling.

Laundry soap nuts

Soap nuts are dried fruit shells harvested from soap berries. They grow on trees in the *Sapindus* genus and contain a natural soap called saponin which is released when it comes into contact with water. They have been used for thousands of years as a natural washing detergent and are available to buy online.

Refill pouches

Refill pouches are a great solution to help reduce single-use plastic waste by reusing laundry bottles in your home. You can purchase refill pouches for both laundry detergent and fabric conditioner so that you use less plastic.

Plastic-free subscription services

There are a number of convenient plastic-free laundry product subscription services that you can now sign up to, delivering both bio and non-bio laundry detergents and fabric conditioners straight to your door. You can tailor the subscriptions to meet your laundry needs, changing how frequently and how much you would like to order. You can even delay your delivery if you are going away or end up having more than you need.

With all of these options now available, what actually makes a credible eco-friendly product? Consider the packaging and whether it is plastic-free or made from 100 per cent recycled plastic and if it can be recycled. It is also worth checking the ingredients and whether they are accredited by any of the trusted bodies such as Cruelty Free International or Allergy UK.

Essential oils

One of the main problems with natural laundry products is that many of them do not have a scent, which is frustrating if you love the fragrance of clean fresh laundry. An easy way to overcome this is by adding essential oils. As I have mentioned before, choosing the scents for my laundry is one of my favourite things to do and getting the right smell can really lift me up on a gloomy day.

Essential oils are a fantastic natural addition to your laundry routine. I absolutely love essential oils as the scents are gorgeous. I find them really enjoyable and comforting to use and I also enjoy experimenting with different scent combinations. Essential oils can also help your wellbeing, with zesty fragrances to boost your energy and relaxing scents to help reduce stress and anxiety. Adding essential oils can have some useful benefits for our wash load too as many of them have natural antibacterial and antimicrobial properties, which is ideal for cleaning our clothes.

How to use essential oils in your laundry

Add a couple of drops of essential oil to your detergent to give it a scent boost by adding to the main wash section of your washing machine drawer.

You can also make your own fabric softener by adding essential oils to white vinegar. Or you could incorporate essential oils into your drying routine by adding a few drops to some woollen dryer balls or a damp cloth and placing in your tumble dryer. They will leave your laundry smelling incredible as the oils will be absorbed by the ball or cloth which will then infuse into your fabrics as they dry. Be careful, though, as essential oils are flammable, so this is only suitable for drying at cooler temperatures, and be sure to purchase good-quality essential oils and not just the fragrance drops. You don't want to cause any discolouration of your laundry by using the latter. Avoid choosing oils that have a natural pigment as this may also discolour fabrics, particularly whites.

Common essential oils and their benefits

Lavender

Widely known for its relaxing properties, this has been used for centuries to prevent the spread of illness and to support the immune system. Lavender is the perfect essential oil to add to your laundry, particularly when washing your bedding to help give you a cosy, restful night's sleep.

Lemon

An invigorating, zesty and fresh scent that is great for energising and disinfecting your laundry. It is also a fantastic stain remover as it contains natural citric acid which dissolves the stain.

Eucalyptus

A great oil to add to your wash during times of sickness. It works as a degreaser, removing stains and getting rid of dirt and any musty odours with its fresh scent. It also kills dust mites and helps to remove allergens in your laundry.

Tea tree

This is fantastic for fighting the growth of mould in your home. A great essential oil to use for keeping your cleaning cloths fresh and ideal for adding to your washing machine cleaning routine. Tea tree oil is great for doing pet laundry or to refresh musty towels as it has a broad range of antimicrobial, antifungal, antiseptic and antiparasitic properties.

Peppermint

A wonderfully invigorating minty scent that helps to stimulate and awaken the mind. Peppermint has antibacterial and antimicrobial properties and is great for using alongside tea tree oil when someone in your home is sick.

Rosemary

A brilliant disinfectant as it has antifungal properties. Team with lemon essential oil for an extra uplifting scent.

Thyme

An essential oil that has been used for many years for its cleaning properties including during the Second World War when it is said to have been used to disinfect hospitals.

Oregano

Another essential oil that has been used historically for its ability both to disinfect and to support the immune system. Use oregano in your washing machine to prevent sickness or to fight a bug in your household.

Geranium

A very calming, relaxing scent that is said to aid circulation.

Laura's little self-care tips

Essential oils and botanicals have been used for over 5,000 years as healing agents. They not only have a beautiful, natural scent but they also have many wellness benefits. Whether it be the soothing scent of lavender on your bed sheets to help you get a good night's sleep or the invigorating minty freshness of peppermint to stimulate your mind, why not try incorporating essential oils as part of your laundry routine and using them to fragrance your home as part of your self-care routine?

It is great to see the variety of sustainable eco-friendly solutions becoming more widely available and I love how innovative many of the solutions are. It's also brilliant to see manufacturers of laundry products taking action to be more conscious, particularly in terms of their packaging and transportation solutions, as this will help considerably in terms of making a difference to the global challenge of sustainability.

Traditional cleaning products like white vinegar and soda crystals as well as essential oils are a must-have for any household. They are a great non-toxic solution for any budget and are readily available. I tend to buy soda crystals and white vinegar in bulk as I use them all the time. They are so useful, not just for my laundry but for other household tasks. My mum always has a little scoop for her soda crystals so of course I now have one too and that makes it easier to dose the powder into the wash.

Although the number of different options can seem overwhelming, hopefully this section has helped to highlight what alternatives you could consider if you haven't already.

Washing — 30 minutes
Drying — 60 minutes
Putting away —
7—10 working days

5

Caring for your fabrics

I absolutely love clothes and I have done since I was little. When I was twelve, I even wrote a letter to the CEO of a large high-street retailer to ask him why there was such a poor selection of stylish clothes for young girls my age! What I love most is wearing clothes that I feel comfortable in – it makes me feel so much more confident even if, over the years, I have made some dodgy style choices (as I'm sure we all have) . . . I'm the kind of gal who, if I find something that I like that fits and makes me feel great, I want it in every colour! I'm not one for designer brands or anything too expensive, I love high-street fashion. But I am also quite picky about the fabrics I wear as I don't like them to feel poor quality or scratchy against my skin and I like them to wash well multiple times without shrinking, bobbling or discolouring.

In a generation of 'fast fashion' I am now becoming much more conscious of the amount of clothes I buy (although my partner Gavin might disagree with this statement!). As I am getting older, I am learning to buy fewer 'on trend' pieces that I might only wear for one season and instead invest in more staple items for my wardrobe that I can mix and match, and wear for years to come.

I also adore having different fabrics to style my home, as I feel that it makes it more cosy and homely. Soft blankets and cushions, fluffy towels and comfy bedding all really help to make a house a home. I think that all of the fabrics in your home that you can touch and feel really help to make you feel soothed and relaxed, so you want them to be fresh, clean and soft.

Laundry symbols: the ultimate guide

Whether it comes to clothes or home fabrics, I find you usually can't go wrong if you follow the garment care instructions on the label, but it can be confusing to know what all of the symbols actually mean. Here then is a handy guide to decode the laundry symbols you might come across so that you can become a laundry care expert! If you like, you can cut this page out of the book and pop it next to your washing machine as a reminder when you're putting your next load on. Alternatively, I've framed mine and put it in my laundry room as I thought it looked cute (as well as being really useful).

Washing symbols

The washing machine sign is like a little tub with water in it and this means that the item can be machine washed using any

Laundry Symbols

WASH MAX 30°C WASH MAX 40°C WASH MAX 60°C DO NOT WASH HAND WASH

MACHINE WASHABLE SYNTHETICS CYCLE GENTLE/WOOL CYCLE DO NOT WRING

IRON MAX 110°C IRON MAX 150°C IRON MAX 200°C DO NOT STEAM DO NOT IRON

TUMBLE DRY LOW HEAT TUMBLE DRY MEDIUM HEAT TUMBLE DRY HIGH HEAT TUMBLE DRY ALLOWED PERMANENT PRESS DELICATE/ GENTLE DO NOT TUMBLE DRY

DRY CLEAN ONLY DO NOT DRY CLEAN ANY SOLVENT ANY SOLVENT EXCEPT TRICHLORO-ETHYLENE PETROLEUM SOLVENT ONLY

BLEACHING ALLOWED USE NON-CHLORINE BLEACH DO NOT BLEACH

detergent. If it has a number inside, this indicates the hottest temperature that the garment can be washed at. If it has a hand inside, then this means that the item can be washed in the machine but only on a hand wash cycle. If it has one line under the tub, then this means it should be washed on a synthetics cycle, and two lines means a gentle wool cycle. If the tub has a cross through it, it cannot be machine washed. A crossed-out twisted symbol means that you should not wring the garment when handwashing.

Ironing symbols

The ironing symbol is easily recognisable as it is a little iron icon. The dots inside the iron indicate the maximum temperature that can be used on the garment. One dot means a maximum of 110°C, two dots means a maximum of 150°C and three dots means a maximum of 200°C. These dots can usually be matched with the symbols on the dial of your iron to help you use the correct temperature. A crossed-out iron with steam means that the item is not suitable for steam ironing, and a crossed out iron means it is not suitable for ironing at all.

Tumble drying symbols

Tumble drying symbols are a square with a circle inside and if your care label has this, then it means that the item is suitable for tumble drying. If it has a cross through it, then it is not suitable for tumble drying. If the symbol has dots inside, then this indicates the most suitable temperature to use, so one dot means a low heat, two dots a medium heat and three dots a high heat. If the symbol has one line beneath it, the fabric has been treated to ensure it does not wrinkle so you should use the permanent press setting on your tumble dryer (and shouldn't iron it). If the symbol has two lines beneath it, it means that the fabric can be tumble dried on the delicate/gentle setting.

Dry cleaning symbols

Dry cleaning symbols can be identified as circles. A simple circle indicates that the item is dry clean only and should not be machine washed. A circle with a cross through it means that it is not suitable for dry cleaning. If the circle has a letter inside it, then this gives advice about what dry cleaning solvents should be used. 'A' is any solvent, 'P' is any solvent with the exception of trichloroethylene (don't worry, your dry cleaner will know what this means!) and 'F' means petroleum solvent only.

Bleaching symbols

Bleaching symbols are triangles. A triangle indicates that the item is suitable for bleaching but if it has a cross through it, then this means that it is not suitable for bleaching. If the triangle has two lines running through it, then this means you should only use non-chlorine bleach.

There are two ways to divide and conquer laundry: by **colour** and **fabric**. But how do you choose which one is more important to prioritise to avoid having to do a million wash loads? Say, for example, you have a white sports bra and the rest of your kit is coloured. In this instance, I would put the coloured kit in together and then pop the white sports bra in with a wash with white towels. Sports kit should not be washed with a fabric conditioner and nor should towels, so this is an ideal solution. I find doing the laundry can be full of puzzles like this. Sometimes you can figure out a savvy solution, but sometimes to avoid having to put on multiple washes you simply have to be patient and not necessarily wash everything straight away.

Sorting clothes by colour

Most of us know that all fabrics should be separated by colour before washing but did you know that the most effective way to do this is whites, lights (neutrals), warms (reds, pinks, oranges), cools (blues, greens) and blacks? It is often overlooked to separate warm and cool tones from black items, putting all darks together, but this can lead to colour bleeding and fabrics losing their brightness, so it is definitely worth considering.

However, let's face it, nobody wants to have to sort their dirty clothes into a million piles of washing and it would be inefficient to only have a few items of each colour in every wash. If this is the situation you face, this is where using colour catcher sheets really comes into its own as it means you can mix loads, even if they contain different tones. Using colour catchers was a game changer for me, as I tend to try to keep it really simple and sort my wash loads by colour into white, lights and darks.

Sorting clothes by fabric

After dividing your clothes by colour, it's worth also thinking about the different fabrics you need to wash. Every fabric contains different fibres which benefit from a certain type of wash. Follow these easy washing tips to help best care for yours. We'll start with natural fabrics:

Cotton

Cotton is one of the most durable natural fibres commonly found in clothing and bedding. Cotton is 100 per cent biodegradable and is also breathable and hypoallergenic so it is used for many everyday items such as T-shirts, underwear and bedding. It is strong and absorbent, but it does often shrink slightly in the first wash as it is a natural fibre that is not very flexible.

Cotton is easy to clean and with a good detergent, washing on cooler temperatures is sufficient and will also help protect the colours. Unless the item is heavily soiled then a 30°C wash should be enough but go slightly higher to remove stains. To prevent shrinking or misshaping cotton items use a slower spin speed to avoid damaging the fibres. The natural cotton fibres can also become tangled in the wash and when they dry become stiff and static so it is important to use a fabric conditioner to keep them soft and smooth so that they continue to feel as comfortable as possible against your skin.

Cotton fabrics can be dried in the tumble dryer, but the constant spinning can cause damage to the fibres so be sure to set your machine to a low spin speed and low temperature to avoid them shrinking or bobbling.

Linen

Linen is a natural fabric that comes from flax, a fibre taken from plants. I purchased my first set of linen bedding for summer this year and oh my goodness, what a treat it is! It is beautiful, so breathable, cool and lightweight. I also love linen shirts and shorts; they are so comfortable to wear even when it is very hot. I think the texture of linen has such a lovely classic timeless summery feel. Lots of tea towels and tablecloths are also made from linen.

Linen actually becomes softer and more absorbent after each wash. Use a low temperature and a mild detergent to protect the fibres. As linen is a natural fabric there will likely be some shrinkage after the first couple of washes but to minimise damage to the fabric avoid using hot temperatures in the washer or dryer. Hang linen items on clothes hangers as soon as they are dry to avoid further wrinkling.

Linen creases very easily so requires ironing. I must admit, I don't tend to iron my linen bedding as I prefer the more casual 'lived in' styling for my bed but anything else will need ironing as otherwise it can look very wrinkled. I use a steam generator iron and it removes the creases in linen wonderfully. I also spritz some crease releaser as I find that helps to remove the wrinkles and it makes the fabric smell divine too.

Silk

Silk is such a luxurious-feeling fabric which is shiny and flexible. It is an animal fibre which retains its shape well and has a high moisture absorbency. I only own a couple of silk items as I tend to avoid buying them, especially if they are dry clean only. You may be surprised that even if you have a silk garment that says 'dry clean' on the label, with care it can be washed at home. I find that many silk dresses and underwear can be washed by hand unless the garment care label states 'dry clean *only*', in which case it is best to follow that. It is always safest to take bright-coloured or printed silks to the dry cleaner's as the rich colours can often bleed. This is also the case with any stains as spot treating on silk can cause a lightening of the fabric so it is always best to handle with care.

Hand wash silk items with care in cool water and use a liquid detergent that is suitable for delicates. Fill your sink or bucket with water and add the detergent, mixing to dissolve the product and create bubbles. Add the item and gently rub using your fingers and swish it through the water, avoiding any scrubbing movements. Wash for a few minutes, rinse well and then very carefully squeeze dry; do not twist or wring silk as you could cause damage. Avoid using the tumble dryer and instead lay silk items out flat on a towel to dry so that they do not become misshapen. Keep them away from direct sunlight as silk colours can fade easily.

Check your garment care label to see if the item can be ironed. If it is suitable for ironing, then turn the item inside out and use a low setting when the silk is still slightly damp. Hang the garment on a padded hanger to retain its shape after ironing.

Wool

Wool is a natural fibre known for its insulating properties, keeping you warm when it's cold. It is also stain-, dirt- and crease-resistant. Wool is a fabric that requires great care to wash and dry as it is prone to shrinking. Woollen items like cashmere and angora can be very expensive, so it is definitely worth being extra careful when washing them. I am actually allergic to wool (as soon as I touch it my skin feels really itchy) so I tend to avoid anything containing wool but for some reason cashmere seems to be fine, most probably because it is much softer against your skin. Typical as it is more expensive!

As wool is such a commonly used fabric in clothing most items can be machine washed. Caring for your cosy woollies is important to keep them fresh but also to avoid shrinkage, damage to the fibres and pilling. Always check the care label and choose a delicate detergent and fabric conditioner. Turn your woollen items inside out before machine washing on a cool, delicate wash cycle. Many machines have a specific wool wash cycle which tends to be a cool wash at a slow spin speed.

Reshape your woollen fabrics straight out of the machine using your hands. Do not wring, stretch or twist the fabric as this may cause items to become misshapen. Woollen items cannot be tumble dried so allow to dry naturally by laying them flat on top of a fresh towel.

Leather

Leather is particularly difficult to give wash advice on as there are so many different finishes so it is important to read the garment care label. If an item is labelled not washable, then always take it to the dry cleaner's to avoid damaging it. If your leather item states that it is washable, then handle with care and I recommend patch testing before you hand wash with a soft wooden brush and soap. There are many leather cleaning and conditioning products available to prolong the life of your leather goods. Personally, I find that due to the nature of leather fabrics most items like jackets, dresses or trousers can be easily freshened by hanging to air and spritzing the lining with a fabric refresher to remove any odours.

You should never wash your leather jacket in the machine as it will result in damage to the fabric. However, to give it a refresh at home you can hand wash the lining using a solution of warm water and a delicate detergent. Turning the garment inside out and using a damp cloth, gently scrub the inside of your jacket, focusing on the areas that will most likely need refreshing like the armpits, collar and cuffs. Ensure all of the traces of soap are removed and hang to dry naturally.

Now, let's move on to synthetic fabrics:

Nylon

Nylon was the first manmade fabric to be developed, and was a revolution in the textiles industry when it was invented in 1938. It is very resistant and flexible, known for its ability to dry quickly, which is why many coats and sportswear items are made from this fabric. Nylon fibres are flexible, strong and often blended with elastane for comfortable, silky garments like hosiery and blouses. The great thing about nylon is that it is also easy to wash on a normal cycle.

Nylon does not shrink in the tumble dryer but you should only iron it if required on a low heat setting as it can melt if it is ironed at higher temperatures.

LAURA'S LITTLE LAUNDRY TIPS
You can purchase mesh bags to pop items in when washing them in the machine. They are really handy for small delicate items like tights and lingerie so that they don't get tangled up or damaged.

Polyester

Polyester came about in the 1940s and is made from plastic, so your shirt and your water bottle are most likely made from the same thing! Did you know that when you recycle plastic it is often melted down to make polyester clothing? The best polyesters hold their shape well and are crease resistant. Polyester fibres dry quickly but they are not as breathable as other fabrics. So many items are now made from polyester as it is durable and lightweight and the great thing is that it is easy to wash.

Use a 30°C wash cycle with similar coloured items and use a fabric conditioner to reduce static on the fabric. Be careful when drying and ironing as polyester can shrink or even melt if the temperature used is too hot. If tumble drying and ironing, use a low heat setting. However, polyester tends to dry naturally quite quickly so hang items straight out of the wash and the creases will drop out without ironing.

Rayon

Rayon is a semi-synthetic fabric that is similar to cotton but it also drapes well and has a soft, silky texture. It is not weakened by chemicals and perspiration and dirt does not cling to it. Rayon isn't a particularly durable fabric, it can be stretched or shrunk in the washing machine and it does tend to yellow with age so hand washing is usually advised using a delicate detergent.

You should not tumble dry items made from rayon as it is prone to shrinking so it is best to dry it in its natural shape or hang it up. To remove creases use a steamer or hover the iron over the item with the steam setting to avoid causing any damage.

Fleece

Fleece is a very popular fabric that was developed in the 1980s. It is made using recycled PET bottles as a base. It is widely used as it is known for keeping you warm so it is usually used in mid layers worn underneath a jacket and also for cosy blankets.

Before washing fleece be sure to close zips to avoid any damage and turn the item inside out to prevent pilling. Select a gentle cycle with a cool temperature and a low spin speed. Ideally a front-loader washing machine should be used as top loaders can often be a little too abrasive. You should never use fabric conditioner when washing fleece items if you want them to stay fluffy. Do not use your tumble dryer; fleece fabric is quick drying so is easy to dry naturally which is why it is so widely used for outdoor and adventure clothing.

Satin

Satin is a luxurious, smooth fabric often used for blouses, dresses, lingerie and premium bedding. A cool hand wash is usually the safest method for washing satin using a delicate detergent. Soak for up to 30 minutes and rinse thoroughly with cool water. Do not use the tumble dryer. Instead, leave the item to dry in its natural shape, and do not wring or twist it. Most likely a satin item will be wrinkly after washing so use a gentle steamer or if using an iron, place a cloth between the garment and the iron to remove the creases safely.

Denim

Denim is a sturdy thick cotton-weave textile that has been used since the mid-nineteenth century. It gained popularity in 1873 when tailor Jacob W. Davis manufactured the first pair of reinforced denim trousers (otherwise known as jeans). They were so popular he then moved production to the facilities of dry goods wholesaler Levi Strauss & Co. Most of us own at least one pair of jeans and there are a few top tips for washing them to help keep their shape and prolong their life:

- Consider washing dark-coloured denim items before their first wearing to avoid dye transfer, which can be impossible to remove from light-coloured items like handbags or upholstery on furniture.
- Wash denim only when it's stained or after multiple wears. Unlike some other fabrics, denim does not require washing after every wear and, in fact, it is actually better for the fabric if you wash it less.
- Turn jeans inside out before washing them to prevent them becoming worn and losing their colour.
- Fasten buttons and zips to avoid any snagging.
- For ripped jeans clip the opening together to prevent them from further fraying or use a laundry bag.
- Use a cool 30°C short delicate cycle (slow spin speed).
- Wash with similar colours to avoid dye transfer.
- Dry your jeans naturally by removing from the washing machine and shaking before hanging which will remove

the creases. To avoid damp pockets dry your jeans inside out. If you do need to tumble dry, then choose a low heat setting. Remove from the dryer when they are slightly damp to reshape and finish drying on a hanger or lying flat.

LAURA'S LITTLE LAUNDRY TIPS
To prevent your favourite black jeans from fading, when you first wash them, turn them inside out before putting into the machine and washing them on a cool setting with white vinegar, which will set the dye and prevent it from bleeding.

Lace

Lace is an elegant fabric that is used for many items including lingerie, dresses, tablecloths, curtains and, of course, bridalwear. Lace is a particularly delicate fabric that should be washed with care. Machine washing is not recommended as this can damage the lace. Instead, hand wash with a delicate detergent and cool water. Soak the item for about 30 minutes and then rinse thoroughly, avoiding any vigorous scrubbing. Do not twist or wring the item as this can stretch the delicate fibres, particularly when they are wet, and lay it out to dry flat in its natural shape. Lace can be ironed using a low heat setting when still slightly damp using a cotton sheet or towel so that the iron does not directly touch the garment. If the garment care label states that the item can be machine washed, then I definitely recommend using a mesh wash bag to protect it and avoid any snagging.

The key to prolonging the life of our fabrics is to ensure that we take care to launder them correctly. I am guilty of ruining (many) garments in the past by not reading the care label and just bunging everything in together and hoping for the best! But it is *so* frustrating when your favourite fabrics get damaged and it could have easily been prevented by washing them correctly.

Caring for the fabrics in our lives is a form of self-care, making us feel warm and comforted. Many of our clothes have memories attached to them and we feel good about ourselves when we are wearing them. Whether it be freshening up your favourite pair of jeans or washing your cosy bed sheets, doing it with consideration and pride will certainly make you feel good and make them last longer at the same time.

Having an empty
laundry basket is the
best 5 seconds of
the week.

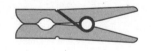

6

The stain removal directory

Stains are one the most annoying laundry problems and I get messages every day from people who need advice and suggestions for removing stubborn stains on their fabrics. So I thought I would dedicate an entire section of this book purely to helping you remove stains. I hope that my stain removal directory will be useful for you to grab for years to come, whenever you are faced with an irritating stain and need a quick solution to help you tackle it with confidence.

Whatever stain you are faced with, do not panic! Don't let the pesky stain get the better of you; no stain is worth your stress. This quick and easy guide will equip you with a solution to confront any stain with confidence and solve the problem.

Stain removal chemistry

Before we get started, I think it is useful to try to understand the science behind stain removal, which has helped me when finding solutions to getting rid of everyday stains on fabrics rather than simply attempting to use any old stain remover on it that I had lurking in the back of the cupboard. Chemistry is certainly not my strong point but hopefully this will help to simplify things.

Oxidisable stains

Oxidisable stains are usually brightly coloured. Examples of oxidisable stains are tea, coffee, red wine, lipstick and fruit juice.

Bleaches are the most effective way of removing oxidisable stains because they turn coloured substances into colourless ones by breaking down their structure. The two main types are oxygen-based bleaches and chlorine-based bleaches.

Chlorine bleach is the most powerful, but it is also more dangerous and toxic so should be used with care. Never mix with other products and wear rubber gloves when using it. It is also important to have good ventilation when using bleach so open windows and doors to allow the circulation of air.

Oxygen-based bleach such as hydrogen peroxide is safer but does not work as effectively below 40°C. Oxi powders are increasingly popular oxygen-based bleach products and I always make sure I have a tub of these in my laundry cupboard as they are so useful for removing everyday stains.

Greasy stains

Greasy stains are also known as surfactant stains. Common examples include grease, butter and oil.

Surfactants like detergents and soap are the best solution for greasy stains as they help dissolve oils in water by lifting the dirt, leaving a spotless surface. Surfactants are the primary component of most laundry detergents due to their ability to trap dirt and lift it from the surface, making stains easier to remove and rinse away.

Particulate stains

Particulate stains like soil and mud are made up of a combination of different elements so this makes it easy for the dirt to infiltrate fabrics and cause staining.

Washing detergent and baking soda, also known as 'builders', are the best way to remove particulate stains and are often added to surfactants to improve their effectiveness. Builders soften water and neutralise any ions.

Enzymatic stains

Enzymatic or protein-based stains include blood, grass, chocolate and eggs. They are strongly influenced by temperature. Enzyme-based cleaners are the most effective way to remove this type of stain because they break down the bond created by the proteins. These cleaners contain different types of enzymes depending on the stain, so proteases break down proteins, amylases break down starches and lipases break down fats.

Most biological laundry detergents are really effective at removing enzymatic stains and I find that particularly the liquid or gel options are very handy as you can use them to pre-treat the stain directly before putting the item into the machine.

The most common stains

The main problem with stain removal is that there are so many different variables including the type of material, whether it be clothing, upholstery or carpet, as well as the length of time it has been left on the fabric. You may find that you come across a stain and you don't even know what it is or how long it has been there. Before reaching for any chemicals, try using a bowl of hot water and a tablespoon of washing-up liquid to see whether this will lift the stain. If this doesn't work, then try a cup of white vinegar in a bowl of warm water.

And again, as a reminder, don't panic! The following section is your encyclopaedia for stain removal. I have explained how I remove the most common household stains in alphabetical order so that you can refer to it whenever you need.

Blood

Bloodstains are one of the most common stains I am asked for advice about, mostly period stains and I'm sure every person who menstruates can relate to this. They are nothing to be embarrassed about and there are many ways they can be tackled.

Bloodstains are protein based and can be even more difficult if left to dry. However, they can be treated using an enzyme-based cleaner. Aim to tackle fresh bloodstains as soon as possible as this will make them far easier to remove.

Firstly, remove any excess blood by rinsing in cold water. Hot water will make the stain worse and cause it to seep deeper into the fabric.

Pre-treat the item by pouring a biological liquid or gel detergent onto the stain. There are also other alternatives like blotting the bloodstain with a small amount of hydrogen peroxide but be careful as this may discolour the fabric so is best really only for lighter colours. You can also mix a baking soda paste (two parts baking soda and one part water) as a pre-treatment.

Put straight into your washing machine without rinsing, add more of the biological detergent to the wash load and put on a wash cycle following the garment care label.

Chewing gum

Chewing gum really is so frustrating (and pretty disgusting) if it gets stuck to your clothes. Place ice cubes on the gum for a couple of minutes then get a sharp knife and separate the gum from the fabric. You can also try putting the item into the freezer to make the gum easier to remove.

Chocolate

I am definitely a chocolate lover and especially if you have children, it is very likely that you will need a solution for removing chocolate stains at some point. No matter how careful I am I always seem to manage to get a chocolate smudge on me when I am wearing white! The mix of fat and sugar means that chocolate stains are best removed using a biological detergent to break down the grease and enzymes.

Pre-treat the stain by blotting it with the detergent and then putting on a wash following the garment care instructions.

Curry

I absolutely love a good curry although I am never very adventurous and always seem to stick to a good old tikka masala or butter chicken. Curry dishes are delicious, bright and aromatic but spilling them can cause some nasty-looking stains due to the spices and oils they contain, which can be tough to tackle but not impossible. Some curry stains can become permanent if not treated quickly.

Mix equal parts washing-up liquid and white vinegar in cold water then apply the solution to the stain with a clean cloth. This should help to break down the oil in the curry. Then to remove the colour staining put it in your washing machine with an oxi powder and a biological detergent.

Deodorant

Deodorant stains can be a pain whether it be marking your little black dress or yellow underarm marks on your favourite shirt. I've always worn strong deodorant since I was a teenager as I feel like I sweat so much and I have found that it is best to prevent deodorant staining particularly white or light-coloured items by washing them as soon as I have finished wearing them, in the summer in particular, to stop any bacteria mixing with the deodorant and causing the yellow marks.

Deodorant stains can be removed using white vinegar. Soak them for an hour or so and then brush the stain with a clean brush (a toothbrush works well) before putting into the machine and washing as normal.

Fruit and fruit juice

Fruit stains are made up of natural colours, sugars and oils so you need a tough detergent to remove them properly. Firstly, rinse the stain using cold water and then pre-treat it using a liquid or gel detergent before popping in your machine on a cool wash cycle.

For particularly bad stains you can also add an oxi powder to the wash to help remove the colouring.

Grass

See Mud and grass, below.

Grease

Greasy stains require a surfactant in order to dissolve and break down the oils. I find that washing-up liquid does a great job of removing grease as it is not only tough on your dishes but also on fabrics. Pre-treat the greasy mark by putting washing-up liquid directly onto the stain before putting into your washing machine with a biological detergent.

Ink

Ink (including permanent marker) can be removed from fabrics by dabbing with rubbing alcohol, cheap hairspray or even hand sanitiser. Providing they contain high levels of alcohol, solvents will dilute and break down the ink stain before you put the item into the washing machine. Before using this method test the garment for colourfastness first using a cotton bud and blotting with kitchen roll. If no colour comes off on the towel, then it should be safe to pre-treat. Place the stain face down onto a cloth or paper towel and use a sponge to apply to the fabric. The ink should loosen and transfer to the cloth beneath.

Lipstick

As with most stains, aim to remove lipstick as soon as possible. Firstly, lay the item stain side down on an old cloth or towel. Blot a liquid detergent on the reverse side of the fabric so that the lipstick transfers onto the cloth beneath. If you rub the stain directly, it is likely to make it worse as the oil and colour will seep deeper into the fabric. Repeat if necessary until you have removed the worst of the stain, then pop into the washing machine with a biological detergent and some oxi powder and the lipstick stain should then be fully removed without a trace.

LAURA'S LITTLE LAUNDRY TIPS
To prevent foundation from transferring onto your clothes prep your skin first using a primer and finish by using a setting spray. You can also spritz your collar with hairspray to stop your make-up from transferring. When I am putting on my make-up I tend to wear my cosy dressing gown to save my clothes, unless I am planning to wear a tight-fitting top, which is always best to put on before applying your make-up.

Make-up

Foundation and make-up stains can be removed by pre-treating with washing-up liquid or a biological laundry detergent. Leave it to sit for about 15 minutes before scrubbing with a clean soft-bristled brush and rinsing in hot water. Put in your washing machine with a biological detergent along with oxi powder following your garment care instructions.

Mould

Black mould spots can appear on fabrics usually if they are left in damp, warm conditions for a long period of time. White vinegar is an excellent solution for removing mould from fabrics as it not only kills the mould but also removes the stain. You can pre-treat the stain by spritzing with a diluted vinegar and water solution in a spray bottle or you can soak the whole item in equal parts water and white vinegar.

You can also wash the item in the machine with a biological detergent and 1 or 2 cups of white vinegar which kills mould and mildew and neutralises any nasty lingering odours.

LAURA'S LITTLE LAUNDRY TIPS
Allow your freshly washed and stain-treated laundry to dry naturally outdoors in the sunshine if possible. The sun's UV rays act as a natural stain remover and will make your whites look brighter.

Mud and grass

Mud and grass stains are usually a sign of fun times, whether it be playing sport, enjoying the great outdoors or pottering around in the garden. They can be removed from your fabrics relatively easily using the following method. Gently rub the stain using a liquid biological detergent and allow to work for a few minutes before washing as usual in your machine.

Nail polish

Nail polish is made up of a variety of chemicals and dyes, hardening into the fabric when it dries and making it difficult to remove. You can remove nail varnish from your clothes by firstly letting it dry. If you try to remove it before it dries, it will go tacky and likely make the stain worse so let it harden before attempting to treat it. Once the nail polish is hard scrape off any excess and then soak a microfibre cloth in an acetone-based nail polish remover and gently dab. I recommend testing this on a less visible part of the item beforehand to check the colourfastness as you do not want to cause any more damage. You must avoid scrubbing or wiping the nail polish as it will only make it seep further into the fabric. Finally, pop into your machine and wash as normal using an oxi powder to remove any discolouration.

Paint

There are two main types of paint – oil-based and water-based. Stains from both types of paint can be removed by soaking using a mixture of half detergent, half warm water. Blot the stain vigorously until the paint has been removed then wash as normal in the machine. If this is not successful, then you could try using acetone-based nail polish remover or rubbing alcohol, applying it gently with a clean toothbrush.

Pet stains

Removing pet stains is something I am very familiar with, having two male dogs. There are various pet stain removal products available to purchase. My favourite comes in a bottle with a brush attached as it is so handy; if you have puppies, it is a must-have. The most important thing to consider when purchasing a pet stain removal product is that it should not have a strong scent as pets are particularly sensitive to odours. I'm sure I read somewhere that a dog's sense of smell is between 10,000 and 100,000 times greater than ours so this is definitely worth being mindful of. I have found that a solution of 50/50 white vinegar and water is fantastic for removing pet stains. It is a natural cleaner so it's non-toxic to pets and neutralises the stains as well as any odours.

The acidic nature of vinegar acts to break down the protein in pet urine. Some products that claim to be pet stain and odour removers may get rid of the stain but may not be sufficient to fully break down the enzymes, resulting in your dogs repeatedly urinating on the same item. Some products may also exacerbate the problem, particularly if they contain bleaches.

Take care when using chemicals around your pets and if you do choose to use a pet stain removal product, then ensure that the cleaned fabric has fully dried before you allow your pet to come into contact with it again.

Poop

Poop will not only leave an unpleasant stain but also a bad smell. To remove poop from fabrics in your washing machine use a biological laundry detergent to lift the stains as this will break down the proteins.

Rinse off as much poop as possible and soak the stained item in warm water. You can pre-treat the stain using a liquid or gel detergent before popping into the washing machine.

Red wine

Red wine is an oxidisable stain that can be removed using bleach which will break down the transferred colour. Before reaching for the bleach, though, try covering the stain in white vinegar which will neutralise the purple and red colour pigments. Immediately after this rub in a liquid or gel laundry detergent and wash the item in the machine on a warm cycle.

Many people swear by using white wine to remove red wine stains but beware as this can often make the problem worse so don't waste a perfectly good glass of wine trying.

Suncream

We all know the importance of wearing suncream to prevent sunburn and skin cancer but removing any stains can be tricky as creams are oil-based so the sun and heat can cause a stain to penetrate the fabric quickly. Washing-up liquid is great for removing suncream stains as it is a relatively strong detergent which dissolves the grease and oils. Pre-treat in warm water and washing-up liquid and let it sit for an hour or so before putting into your washing machine with a biological detergent. White vinegar and eucalyptus oil are also great at pre-treating suncream stains before you wash your clothes as normal.

Sweat

Sweat stains usually appear over time in the armpits of your favourite shirts and can cause a yellowing of the fabric. They can be removed by soaking the garment in white vinegar for an hour and then gently scrubbing with a clean brush. Once you have finished, wash in your machine as usual. Try adding an oxi powder to the wash which will help to restore your bright whites and refresh colours.

Tea and coffee

Try to remove tea and coffee stains when they are fresh before the particles have set into the material. Immediately run through cold water but do not scrub. If this does not completely remove the tea or coffee stain, then add a few drops of laundry detergent and gently rub before putting into your washing machine with an oxi powder alongside a biological detergent. You can get oxi powders for both whites and colours and check the instructions on the packaging for the correct dosage. I don't know why but whenever I am travelling on the train to London I grab a coffee and I always seem to spill a bit down me. I always have to go to the toilet to rinse it off so end up with an embarrassing wet patch!

Tomato sauce

Tomato-based sauces and ketchup are another really common stain. I love a good spaghetti bolognese but inevitably I will end up with sauce down me.

Remove any excess sauce, blot with a clean cloth, cold water and a teaspoon of liquid detergent before putting the garment into your washing machine following the care instructions on the garment label.

Urine

Most urine stains, whether it be human or pet urine, can be removed from clothing and bedding using a normal wash cycle as long as you select a biological detergent that can break down the enzymes. If it is an old stain, then treat by mixing a stain remover using equal parts hydrogen peroxide, baking soda and washing-up liquid in a spray bottle. You can also use this mixture to remove urine stains on mattresses.

With two male puppies I am finding that I am having to tackle their urine stains more often than I would like at the moment. The main thing I have found is that you need to completely remove all of the urine using a biological detergent or the naughty little monkeys will just continue to mark their scent in the same place.

Vomit

Getting rid of vomit stains is not a nice task since it usually has an unpleasant smell and looks pretty disgusting too. Try to tackle the stain as soon as possible as this will make it far easier to remove.

Rinse the stain with warm water, which may be sufficient to remove the vomit and the stain if done quickly. If you can't treat the item straight away, then try to at least soak it in warm water as this will prevent the stain from drying and becoming more stubborn to remove when you do have the time to tackle it.

If rinsing the stain is not sufficient to remove it, then pre-treat the garment with a biological laundry detergent before putting it into the washing machine on a warm wash cycle.

Wax

I am obsessed with my cosy candles and wax burner; not only do they smell divine but they instantly help me to relax and I feel that they make the house more homely. However, accidents do happen and if wax drips onto your clothes, then you can remove it using the following methods.

I know for every other stain I have said that you should act quickly to help remove it, but it is the opposite with wax. Allow it to dry naturally before attempting to tackle it.

Once the wax is dry, scrape off as much residue as possible which will remove the top layers, leaving you with only the wax that has dissolved into the fabric. The trick to removing the remaining wax is to heat it by placing in underneath a paper towel and ironing over it. This will melt the wax and it will be absorbed into the paper towel on top of it.

If the wax has left a coloured residue on the item, then pre-treat with a biological laundry detergent and wash in the machine on a normal cycle. You may want to add an oxi powder to the wash to help refresh the colour.

Hopefully these tips will have covered everything to help you in times of need when you have a laundry stain emergency but by all means, if you have another stain that is not covered, then feel free to message me on social media and I will try my best to help you with a solution.

Here are my top three tips for tackling almost any stain with confidence so that you can spot it, treat it, soak it and solve it with zero stress.

1. Aim wherever possible to remove stain as soon as you can so that they do not have time to soak into the fabric.

2. You don't need lots of fancy stains removers. A biological liquid or gel detergent, washing-up liquid, white vinegar, soda crystals and an oxi powder are the main items that you need in your laundry cupboard. These products will remove the majority of everyday stains.

3. Always follow the garment care instructions to avoid any damage to the fabric.

Laundry schedule:
Sort — today
Wash — later
Fold — eventually
Iron — ha ha

7

Creating a laundry routine

Rituals help me incredibly day to day, especially if I am having an anxious time. You may be able to relate to having those unexpected sensations of a cloudy head, a sick feeling in your tummy and not being able to think clearly for no reason. During these times, I find that having rituals enables me to take back control and not let anxiety have a hold on me and my day. In this chapter I want to share with you my laundry routine and how it helps me on a daily and weekly basis, as well as throughout the year, so that you can start working towards creating your own. Every household is different and depending on how many people live in your home, you'll have different priorities. Hopefully me sharing my routine will help you find one that works for you.

My daily routine

I tend to put a wash load on every day, which may seem excessive for a household of just the two of us, but I'll explain how I sort my laundry and hopefully it will all become clear!

I sort my laundry into whites, lights and darks then knitwear/ delicates and sportswear. Every day I will tackle whatever has built up the most. So, on a Monday there might be lots of dark items so I pop on a dark wash. Tuesday it might be lots of knitwear and so I might wash these, depending on how many items have built up in the basket. I don't like to put on a wash if there are only a few items as I don't want to be wasteful, but it does then feel like my laundry basket never seems to be empty! I use the colour catcher cloths which I find really help to wash mixed loads without the colours running but I still don't mix lights and darks.

As I work from home, I tend to put a wash on first thing in the morning but in my previous job I used to always put one on in the evening as soon as I got home. If your washing machine has a timer, you could set it so that it finishes first thing in the morning when you get up. Do whatever works for you but the most important thing is that you are able to remove the washing from the machine as soon as possible when the cycle finishes, so you can either hang it up to dry naturally or use the tumble dryer. Usually at the end of the day once everything is dry, I will then take it upstairs and immediately sort all of the clean items into piles ready to be put away. If I don't do this before I go to bed, then I find that I put it off for ages and it disrupts my routine for the next day as I can't start a new load until the basket full of clean items is empty ready to transport the next lot of dirty items to the machine.

LAURA'S LITTLE LAUNDRY TIPS

One item that we often forget to clean is our laundry baskets. I don't tend to see the bottom of mine very often but every now and then I will clean it using an all-in-one disinfectant spray to get rid of the bacteria lurking in there that have accumulated from all of the dirty washing. All-in-one sprays are suitable on many different materials, including fabrics, so are great for baskets that are lined. Leave it to air dry so that it will be germ-free and smelling fresh.

My weekly routine

On a weekly basis I put wash loads on for bedding and the towels that have accumulated over the week. I wash our bedding weekly, usually at the weekend so that it is lovely and fresh to start the new week. Towels can be cleaned every 3–4 days and do not have to be washed daily unless they are particularly dirty. I also wash the bath mats weekly with the towels.

Once a week I will wash all of the cloths that I have used for cleaning along with the tea towels that have accumulated throughout the week. I don't know what it is about a tea towel, but I just think they are so homely. I have a couple of caddies in my laundry room that I put the dirty cloths in; I tend to use quite a lot of cloths because I reach for them as an alternative to disposable cleaning wipes as they are much better for the environment. I put them on to wash with a detergent and replace the fabric conditioner for a laundry cleanser to give them a deep clean and remove any bacteria or viruses.

LAURA'S LITTLE LAUNDRY TIPS

A small simple switch that I have made is making my own cleaning cloths using microfibre cloths and disinfectant. It's so easy to do and is much better for the environment. You can buy plain microfibre cloths in the supermarket or online, and use with your normal cleaning products. Every week I will wash all of my dirty homemade cloths in the machine using a detergent and I swap fabric conditioner for a laundry cleanser or disinfectant to get rid of the germs and bacteria.

Creating a laundry routine

Here's a table showing how I've created my routine:

Daily washes	Weekly washes
When: morning, 5 days a week	When: once a week
Things I'll wash: everyday clothes	Things I'll wash: bedding, towels, bath mats, tea towels, cleaning cloths, dog beds, dog blankets
How I'll organise: divide by whites, lights and darks; and knitwear/delicates and sportswear	How I'll organise: separate according to use: kitchen, bathroom, cleaning, pet bedding

On the opposite page, you'll find space to create your own laundry routine which you can photograph or tear out to pin somewhere useful. I'd love to see what routine works for you, so please do take a photo and share with me online @lauracleanaholic #LiveLaughLaundry

As much as I love a routine, I am also quite a laidback person and I don't put any pressure on myself if I don't rigidly stick to my routine. I am in control of my routine and make it work to help me; I don't let my routine control me, if that makes sense. Let's face it, there's always going to be laundry and if a couple of days go by and I haven't had a chance to do any wash loads, then it's really not the end of the world. I just have a reset and get back on it another day.

Daily washes	Weekly washes
When:	*When:*
Things I'll wash:	*Things I'll wash:*
How I'll organise:	*How I'll organise:*

Laundry

[lôn – drē] noun

Sorting life's problems
one load at a time.

PART 2

Next-level
laundry

8

Laundry gadgets

I am a huge fan of gadgets for cleaning and laundry simply because they make life so much easier and more fun at the same time. If you find a gadget that you enjoy using and that simplifies a task that you usually dread, then the likelihood of you doing that task will increase as you will be more motivated to tackle it.

I think that a good gadget should solve a problem and simplify it with a practical solution to aid our laundry routines, so here's a guide to some of my favourites that I hope you will find useful:

Bobble remover

I have only recently discovered these and I can't believe I never had one before! A bobble remover basically shaves all of the bobbles off your clothes and it works so well, I find it really helps to revive them. I use mine mainly on sweatshirts and jumpers if ever they go slightly bobbly after being in the washing machine.

Clothes folder

I have worked in retail since the age of 17, and one of my first jobs was in a menswear department folding the polo shirts and jeans. It was such a satisfying job folding them all neatly and making them look tidy. We always had a folding table which was a really simple design and helped to make the edges fold neatly – a clothes folder is basically a small household version of that. Folding your clothes neatly reduces creasing and uses much less space in your cupboards, also making clothes far easier to find. I've also seen clothes folders that store the item as well as folding it and they look really organised.

Collapsible laundry basket

A collapsible laundry basket is basically a laundry basket that you can fold down when you're not using it. They are great for saving space as they can be stored away without taking up too much room. They are also ideal for taking camping.

Drying rack

There are so many different drying racks available to suit your space to help make drying your clothes indoors easier. Here in the UK we tend to get lots of rain so having an indoor airer to fit everything on to dry is a must. I have a pop-up airer which is basically like a mini washing line and I love it because you can use it indoors and outdoors too. We also like going away in our campervan so it's really handy for taking away with us to hang towels and swimwear up to dry on. The only downside is that you probably need two of them depending on how much laundry you do but the handy size means that they are really easy to store away when not in use. You can get drying racks that attach to your radiators, ones that you attach to the wall that pull out . . . There are so many different styles so you will be able to find one that suits your space. There are also heated drying racks which are a great alternative if you do not have a tumble dryer.

Handheld fabric steamer

A handheld fabric steamer is a portable plug-in device that you use to steam fabrics. I find mine really useful for bulky items like coats, delicate items like dresses or items that may be awkward to iron. It is great for removing creases from items without having to drag out your iron and ironing board. I like using mine for bedding as you can remove the creases while it is dressed on your bed. I also use mine for freshening up curtains and cushions in between deep cleans. In addition, the steam kills bacteria so it's great for freshening up items that are awkward to wash and you can pack it in your suitcase to use when you are travelling.

Laundry bags

Laundry bags are mesh bags that you can use to put your delicates like lingerie inside and zip close so that they can be safely washed in your machine. The mesh fabric allows the items to be washed effectively without them getting damaged or tangled up with other items in the wash cycle. They are available in different shapes and sizes to suit the items you want to protect including circular ones which are great for bras, stopping them from losing their shape. You can also get special pet laundry bags which are similar but are made with a slightly different fabric to trap the pet hair and stop it clogging up your machine.

Laundry basket for whites, darks and delicates

A laundry basket with three separate sections for lights, darks and delicates is really useful for making it easier to sort your washing. You can see at a glance how much is in each section and put a wash on when there is enough to fill your machine.

Laura's little self-care tips

If you can, invest in a cute laundry basket. I love the aesthetic of a good basket and I know it might sound crazy but if you buy one that you love, subconsciously you will not hate looking at your laundry basket, even if it is overflowing! I used to have one with a lid that slammed shut every time I opened it and it was so frustrating. Even though it was only a small annoyance I realised it was hindering my laundry ritual right from the beginning, making me put off even opening the basket, let alone putting on a wash!

Laundry trolley

A trolley is a great way to store your laundry products to keep them handy, particularly if you don't have a lot of cupboard space. I have seen some great trollies that slide in next to your washing machine, making it really easy to pull out the products you need when you need them.

Lint remover

Lint removers are rollers with sticky paper on them that pick up dust and hairs from your fabrics. Simply roll the sticky paper over your clothes and it will pick up the particles. It is such a handy thing to have for dark items where lint is easily visible as well as coats and jumpers. They are also useful to pack if you are travelling. They are ideal not just for your laundry but I love using them all around the home for dusting too.

LAURA'S LITTLE LAUNDRY TIPS

A lint remover is a great little tool that can be used not only for removing lint from your laundry but I also love to use it all around my home. They are great for removing dust and hair from your sofa, curtains, headboard and lampshades.

Portable ironing blanket

A portable ironing blanket is an ideal alternative to an ironing board. It is a heat-reflective blanket that you can lay out on a table or any other flat, even surface to iron on.

Portable textile refresher

Using plasma technology, portable textile refreshers are small gadgets that can be used to freshen up fabrics when you might not have access to a washing machine. They remove unwanted odours as well as bacteria and viruses to give your clothes a refresh on the go. As they are a relatively new-to-market gadget they are still quite expensive, but they are really useful if you travel a lot.

Portable washing machine

I have seen a few different portable washing machines, but never actually used one myself so would love to know if they are any good. They are basically a mini washing machine that you fill with water and it spins the items. I think that they would be really useful for camping, washing smaller items or if you are living in student accommodation with no access to a washing machine. Some of them plug into the mains or a USB socket but some are hand powered so better for the environment and ideal if you do not have access to electricity while camping. I have also seen a mini turbine that you plug in and attach to a bucket to wash your clothes, but it doesn't get great reviews and I'm not really sure how successful this would be for washing more than one item.

Sock locks

Why is it that socks tend to go into the washing basket in pairs and then disappear never to be found again? Sock locks are a great gadget as you hook your socks onto them so that they go in and come out of the washing machine in pairs. You can get individual ones to clip in a pair of socks or a long stick that you can attach a few pairs to which I think is a great idea so that your socks never go missing again.

Tabletop ironing board

The disadvantage of having an ironing board is that it is big, bulky and you need somewhere to store it away when not in use. Therefore, a tabletop ironing board is really handy if you are short on space and easy to grab whenever you need it. The only downside is that because they are small they are not really suitable for ironing big or bulky items, but they are useful for ironing everyday things.

Tumble dryer balls

Tumble dryer balls are made from either wool or plastic and are used to put into your tumble dryer to help aid the circulation of heat in the machine. This reduces drying time and the wool balls help to absorb excess moisture. They also reduce static and creasing in the tumble dryer as they stop the items tangling up together in the machine.

These are just a few laundry gadgets that are available on the market to help make our lives easier and make washing our clothes as simple as possible whether we are at home or on the move. I am always on the hunt for new gadgets so if there are any that I have missed out or you think I should give a try, then let me know by tagging me on socials with #LiveLaughLaundry @lauracleanaholic.

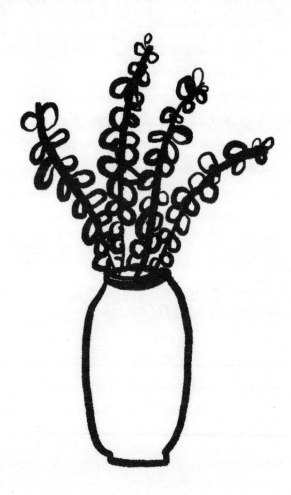

Why do I expect to wake up every day thinking I can conquer the world, when I can't even conquer my laundry?

9

Seasonal laundry tasks

There are many items that I do not clean as part of my daily or weekly laundry routine, so I tend to wash them seasonally, depending on the weather at that time of year, and then keep them smelling fresh in between by using a fabric refresher. They are usually items that are bulky and more difficult to wash and dry, so are not as easy to do as often. I find that doing them seasonally helps to get them done in a more realistic timeframe.

Tasks to complete each season (every 3 months)

Duvets and pillows
Duvets and pillows should ideally be washed every 3–6 months in order to keep them fresh, hygienic and to prevent any dust mites. There's nothing better than snuggling into bed with freshly washed bedding and it definitely helps me to get a better night's sleep, too.

When I shared this on my Instagram reels lots of people said that they just throw theirs away and buy new ones, so hopefully if I explain how to wash them this will save money and reduce the amount of pillows going to landfill.

Washing your pillows

Here are my top tips for washing your pillows:

- Keep your pillows in a pillowcase in the washing machine to avoid them ripping.
- Wash two pillows at a time to balance the load.
- Use your normal detergent and then replace fabric conditioner with vinegar to keep the pillows fluffy and neutralise any odours.
- Use the delicate cycle on your washing machine.
- Add an extra spin after the main wash to speed up the drying process.
- Ensure you allow the pillows to dry fully to avoid any bacteria or mould growing. Give them a good fluff up before allowing to dry naturally or most are suitable for tumble drying.

You can also use these tips for washing scatter cushions; just be sure to read the care label to ensure that they are suitable for machine washing.

Laura's little self-care tips

I love to use a sleep spray on my pillows before I go to bed as I find that it really helps me to relax and fall asleep more easily. There are lots of gorgeous-smelling pillow sprays available to buy but it is also really easy to make your own by mixing a few drops of lavender essential oil with water in a spray bottle and spritzing generously before bed.

Pillows are very personal items and crucial to a comfortable night's sleep and our overall wellbeing. They ideally should be washed 2–4 times a year, but then replaced every couple of years. There are a few signs that it might be time to change yours.

- Your pillow should bounce back when folded. If it stays flat when folded in half, then it is definitely time to replace it.
- If you regularly wake up sneezing, then this could be a sign of dust mites. I am asthmatic and am particularly sensitive to dust so washing and replacing my pillows regularly really helps reduce any allergic reactions.
- If your pillows smell bad even after you have washed and dried them.
- If your pillow has noticeable lumps and bumps that you can't shake out.

- If your skin becomes irritated. Oil, dead skin and dirt can build up on our pillows so if you find that your skin is becoming irritated, then your pillow could be the culprit.
- If you suffer with neck and shoulder pain in the morning, this could be a sign that your pillow needs replacing.

Washing your duvet

Washing a duvet can be a little more challenging than pillows as it is bulkier but by keeping it fresh and clean, you will help ensure your duvet lasts longer. We have a lightweight summer duvet and a warmer winter duvet, so I wash them twice each, at the start and end of the seasons. There's no need to wash them more frequently as they will actually wear out quicker by doing this. Airing your duvet is usually sufficient to keep it fresh and the easiest way to do this is when you are washing your bedding. Allow the duvet to breathe by hanging it on a washing line, or I know many people who hang it on their bannister.

You can wash most duvets in the machine, providing the drum is big enough. A 7kg drum can comfortably wash a duvet for a double bed. If it is crammed in too tightly, it will not wash effectively so dry cleaning is the alternative. Use your non-biological detergent and then replace fabric conditioner with vinegar to keep the duvet fluffy and neutralise any odours. Use the delicate cycle on your washing machine and add an extra but gentle spin after the main wash to speed up the drying process.

To remove any stains from your duvet ideally treat the affected area as soon as possible. Shake the filling away from the stain and then apply the appropriate stain remover depending on what it is before washing as above.

Ensure that your duvet is fully dried before using it to avoid it smelling musty. Many duvets can be dried in the tumble dryer but be sure to check the care label to see if yours is suitable. The best option as always is to allow it to dry naturally outside. Give it a good shake when you remove it from the washing machine to fluff it up and allow the fibres to separate from each other. It is also worth turning your duvet regularly while it is drying to ensure that it keeps its shape.

Blankets

I absolutely love my cosy blankets and throws. They not only keep us warm and snug while we are sat on the sofa watching our favourite TV shows, but they are also a really easy way to style a room to make it feel more homely. It is important to keep them smelling fresh and clean as they do collect dust and allergens, even more so if you have pets who also like a cosy blanket. I tend to wash mine every couple of weeks and rotate them as I do have quite a few, especially having the dogs. It's such a lovely feeling wrapping yourself up and relaxing; it's one of my favourite things to do but the moment wouldn't be quite the same with a musty-smelling blanket! Most blankets can be machine washed on a cool cycle with a mild non-bio detergent. Many blankets contain a high wool content so a cool wash is a must as is a delicate spin to reduce any damage being caused to the fabric. I like to use a little fabric conditioner as it is so good to get a whiff of a lovely scent when you snuggle into the blanket. Some fabric conditioners can cause a build-up on certain blankets so replace with white vinegar in the drawer to restore the fluffiness.

It is best to give blankets a good shake as soon as they come out of the machine to help keep them fluffy and I prefer to allow them to dry naturally although some can be tumble dried.

Tablecloths

I only own a couple of tablecloths that I get out for Christmas, although I must admit, I do love a good tablecloth as I think that they can dramatically change the whole look of your table setting. I would really like to find some more but, if I'm honest, with it just being the two of us at home, we don't tend to eat at the dining table very often. We will either sit on the bar stools on the island in the kitchen or just be TV dinner heads and eat on the sofa! I do love setting the table for Christmas, though, or if we are having family and friends around for dinner, so on those occasions I will freshly wash a tablecloth ready for the meal.

Tablecloths can be machine washed on a cool temperature with a mild detergent. Allow them to dry naturally and then iron so that they look lovely and pressed. I also like to use a crease releaser on the tablecloth as it really helps to remove the creases, especially if you don't have time to iron. I just lay the tablecloth and then give it a spritz and smooth out the creases; your guests will never know!

Curtains

Curtains are such a bulky yet delicate item and should be washed with special care. Curtains should ideally be cleaned once or twice a year depending on how dirty they become. I have totally destroyed a pair of curtains before by not washing them with care, so I definitely recommend that you check the care label before you wash yours.

I recently discovered that my puppies Luther and Enzo were weeing on the curtains across the patio doors in our living room (marking their scent!) so I asked my followers on Instagram for advice about whether or not I could wash them at home or did I need to take them to the dry cleaner's. Everyone said that I could wash them at home so thanks to their advice, this is how I do it.

Many curtains can be machine washed on a cool, delicate cycle with a slow spin speed but if in doubt, then hand wash them to avoid causing any damage. As curtains are usually large, heavy fabrics I hand wash them in the bath as it makes it so much easier and less messy. Fill the bathtub with warm water and a non-bio detergent, then gently wash each section of the curtains.

Curtains will take a long time to dry, so I will only ever wash them on a warm summer's day to help speed up the drying process or they can become musty if they take too long to dry. Hang them to dry on the washing line avoiding direct sunlight as this may discolour the fabric. One of my lovely followers also suggested hanging them back up on the curtain rail to dry and the creases will drop out too.

Net curtains can become particularly dusty and dirty due to the nature of the fabric. They also tend to discolour so to reduce any yellowing of the netting add an oxi stain-remover powder along with the detergent. Net curtains can be machine washed on a cool, delicate cycle but to protect the fabric wash them in a laundry bag or pillowcase to avoid them getting damaged.

LAURA'S LITTLE LAUNDRY TIPS

As washing curtains is not an easy task, I recommend maintaining them so that you don't have to resort to washing them as frequently. Every week, vacuum them using the nozzle attachment to remove any dust and allergens. I also highly recommend investing in a steam cleaner as they are so useful for keeping curtains clean without having to wash them. Any type of steam cleaner will do, but the handheld garment steamers I find are the most convenient for this task. The steam kills any bacteria which is usually also the source of bad odours. I also like to freshen my curtains using a fabric refresher; giving them a regular spritz helps to keep them smelling clean.

Shoes

Many types of shoes can be washed in the machine depending on what fabric they are made from. Shoes like trainers that are made from cotton, nylon, polyester, PU and PVC can all be washed using the washing machine. Fabrics like leather or suede *cannot* be washed in a machine as they can be damaged with water so should be cleaned with products made specifically for that fabric or by a professional.

Always read the care label but usually, even if the fabric states hand wash only, you can still use your washing machine but only on the hand wash setting.

I wear my Converse all the time and have washed them in the machine for years. No matter how muddy or mucky your shoes might be looking, give washing them a go instead of throwing them away as you might be surprised at how it brings them up like new. Here's a beginner's guide to washing your shoes in your washing machine:

- Firstly, remove the laces. I pre-soak these in a washing-up bowl with warm water and an oxi whitening powder before putting them in the machine. Often just removing and washing the laces can really freshen up dirty shoes.
- Rinse the shoes under a cold tap to remove any surface mud and dirt and then wipe with a cloth. I then use a toothbrush to remove any remaining dirt and a cotton bud

or cocktail stick to get rid of any debris that is trapped in the sole or under the lace holes. Preparing your shoes this way will give you better results when washing them in your washing machine.

✦ Put the shoes and laces in a pillowcase or laundry bag and add towels to the drum to avoid them rattling around making a noise in the machine and potentially getting damaged or even damaging your machine.

✦ Use a normal laundry detergent on a cool wash cycle to avoid colours fading.

✦ Allow the shoes to dry naturally as they could lose their shape and the heat from the tumble dryer will likely cause the glue to melt. Ideally dry outdoors, avoiding direct sunlight, and use a clean dry microfibre cloth or scrunch up some newspaper inside the shoe to absorb the water and help them keep their shape.

Rugs

Rugs should be washed twice a year to keep them clean and smelling fresh but as they are quite bulky it is best to wash them on a warm day so that they can dry thoroughly outside and not become musty.

Small cotton and synthetic rugs can be washed in the machine on a cool, delicate setting and air dried. Any stains should be pre-treated depending on the fabric and the stain.

Larger rugs that are too big for the washing machine can still be cleaned relatively easily, but I definitely recommend doing this job outdoors on a warm day so that they can dry effectively. This is how I clean our rugs that can't go in the washing machine:

1. Vacuum the rug on both sides to remove as much loose dirt and dust as possible.

2. Use either a carpet shampoo or mix warm water with washing-up liquid or a non-bio laundry liquid detergent and gently scrub a small area to spot test for colour fastness. If the colour does not bleed, then use a sponge to apply the mixture and give it a good scrub.

3. Wipe with a clean, damp cloth to remove any soap residue.

4. Use a bath towel to soak up any excess moisture.

5. Allow to dry fully, avoiding direct sunlight.

For rugs containing wool, follow the same process but be sure to use cool water and a laundry liquid designed for wool fabrics.

With the two dogs our rugs get an absolute pounding so to maintain them and keep them smelling fresh in between deep cleans, I vacuum them regularly and now and again sprinkle over bicarbonate of soda, leave for an hour or so to allow the bicarb to neutralise any odours and then vacuum up.

Tasks to complete in autumn/winter (cooler months)

As I am such a homebody, I absolutely love the cosiness of the autumn and winter seasons here in the UK when the temperature drops. Long chilly dog walks wrapped up all warm and snug are one of my favourite things to do and having clean items to keep me cosy and smelling clean is also very comforting.

Winter coats and fleeces

I like to wash my winter coats and fleeces at the start of the season after they have been stored away for the summer. Often people avoid washing their coats because they don't want to damage them, but it is easier than you might think to keep yours clean and smelling fresh. Be sure to check the care label and if it does state dry clean only, then it is always best to follow that guidance. If not, then depending on the type of fabric, you can probably wash your coat in the machine.

Wool coats

Since wool is known for its insulating properties it's no surprise that it's used to make many coats. If the care label for your woollen coat does not state dry clean only, then you can wash it in the machine by following these steps:

1. Using a soft brush, use downward strokes to remove any loose dust or dirt.

2. Turn the coat inside out and place inside a laundry bag to protect it in the machine.

3. Wash on a wool cycle using a detergent suitable for wool on a cool temperature with a gentle spin.

4. Allow to dry naturally by reshaping and placing flat on an airer.

Down coats

Down is becoming increasingly popular for winter coats as it is so warm and lightweight but down coats can also be expensive so need to be washed with care in the machine as long as the care label does not state dry clean only.

1. Place in a laundry bag to avoid any snagging to the coat during washing in the machine.

2. Add a detergent suitable for washing down.

3. Add a couple of tennis balls to the washing machine cycle.

4. Wash on a cool temperature with a gentle spin cycle.

5. Dry in the tumble dryer using a low heat and by adding tumble dryer balls to help circulate the heat and restore fluffiness to the down.

6. Remove the coat from the tumble dryer while it is still slightly damp to avoid any heat damage or shrinkage, then give it a good shake and hang to dry fully.

Faux fur

Many winter coats have a faux fur trim which is really cosy and keeps off the wind chill but can get matted and look less fluffy over time. Remove the faux fur if possible and soak for ten minutes in cool water with a tablespoon of detergent. Squeeze and dry using a towel to remove any excess moisture then give it a good shake, leaving it to dry naturally. Finally, brush to refluff.

Ski suits

We have never been skiing but it's something we definitely want to learn to do as it seems like such a fun sport and lots of our family and friends really enjoy it. It is important to wash your ski gear to preserve its lifespan and functionality and to restore breathability and any water-repellent treatments. The majority of ski coats can be washed in the machine and the water-repellent treatment on the fabric can also be restored easily.

1. Empty all pockets and close zips and Velcro to avoid the fabrics being damaged in the wash.

2. Turn the garment inside out (unless it has a waterproof Gore-Tex membrane which is on the inside of the item).

3. Use a liquid detergent on a cool wash cycle with a gentle spin but do not use fabric conditioner. If the ski suit contains down, then it is worth adding a couple of tennis balls to the drum of the machine.

4. After the main wash and spin add an additional rinse and spin cycle to ensure all detergent has been washed through – this also aids the drying process.

5. Hang to dry naturally in a well-ventilated room or use a low heat setting in the tumble dryer for about 45 minutes. The tumble dryer will reactivate any water-repellent coating on the fabric and fluff up the fibres. If drying naturally, then the water-repellent coating can be restored by placing a towel on the garment and running an iron over it a few times.

Fleeces

Fleece is a fantastic insulating fabric so is used for lots of base layer clothing and jackets. It is easy to wash in a machine.

1. Close all zips to stop them getting damaged or snagging the fabric.

2. Turn the fleece inside out to prevent bobbling.

3. Use a cool, gentle wash cycle adding a non-biological detergent and do not use fabric softener as this may damage the fibres.

4. Stains can be removed by blotting with water and rubbing a little washing-up liquid onto the affected area before washing.

5. Line dry either outdoors or in a well-ventilated room. Do not tumble dry or use a radiator to dry fleeces.

Hats, gloves and scarves

We often forget to wash our hats, gloves and scarves but they can become musty smelling if not cleaned. My hats and scarves always tend to get make-up on them so I do wash them more regularly than once a season.

1. Wash in the machine on a delicate cycle using a detergent suitable for wool.

2. Use a laundry bag or a pillowcase to prevent items from tangling up.

3. Remove from the machine as soon as the cycle has finished and reshape them gently.

4. Lay on a towel to air dry as these items are not suitable for the tumble dryer.

Comforters and teddies

Soft toys usually go on lots of adventures, picking up dirt and germs along the way. My brother, sister and I always had our comforters with us, and I remember before we went on holiday each year my mum would always give them their bath before we went away so they were all fresh and clean. If your child is sick, they should definitely be washed then. Most soft toys can be washed in the machine but older, more delicate toys should be hand washed.

Machine washing soft toys:

1. Use a cool, gentle wash cycle with a mild detergent suitable for wool. Add a laundry cleanser as this will kill any lingering bacteria and viruses, even on a cool wash, which is particularly useful if your child has a sickness bug and means you don't have to waste money or energy on a hot wash.

2. Pop the soft toys in a laundry bag or pillowcase to protect them.

3. Add towels to bulk out the drum to prevent the toy from rattling around and potentially getting damaged.

4. Allow to dry naturally. The heat in the tumble dryer can damage any glued parts.

5. If the fur is matted, then use a hair dryer on a low setting to fluff it back up again.

Hand washing soft toys:

1. Soak for 10 minutes in cool water with a tablespoon of mild detergent suitable for wool.

2. Do not wring as this may damage the toy. Instead, squeeze it gently to remove the water.

3. Allow to dry naturally and use a hair dryer on a low setting to fluff up the fur if it is matted.

Tasks to complete in spring/summer (warmer months)

When the sunshine comes out here in the UK I like to make the most of it as it doesn't usually last for long! I really enjoy being outdoors, having trips in our campervan, barbecues with my family and walking along the beach with the dogs. I am always so thankful for the warmer weather when it comes to doing my laundry as it makes it so much easier to get everything dry quickly!

Swimwear

Swimwear fabrics should be treated with care. It is always best to hand wash them as they can sag and stretch out of shape easily. Follow these steps to ensure your swimwear lasts well.

1. Rinse after every swim to avoid damage to the fabric caused by chlorine, sweat, salt and suncream.

2. Hand wash by soaking in cool water with a non-biological detergent. Do not use fabric conditioner. If using the hand wash setting on your washing machine, then place your swimwear in a laundry bag to protect it and prevent it from getting tangled.

3. Dry flat on a towel in the shade, avoiding direct sunlight as this can fade the fabric. Avoid hanging or wringing swimwear as this can cause it to sag and stretch. Do not be tempted to dry swimwear in the tumble dryer.

Baseball caps

Baseball caps are great for keeping the sun off your head and also covering up those bad hair days, but they should not be washed in the machine.

1. Hand wash baseball caps by soaking in cool water with a non-biological detergent.

2. Rinse thoroughly with cool water.

3. Pat dry with a clean towel.

4. Reshape and allow to dry naturally. Stuff with a towel or lay on a small bowl to ensure that the cap dries in shape. You should never dry a baseball cap in the tumble dryer.

Beach towels

To wash your beach towels, shake off as much sand as possible to avoid this going into your machine. If you have damp sand on your towel, then allow it to dry before shaking it off. Set the machine on a normal wash cycle and replace fabric conditioner with white vinegar to keep the towels fluffy. It is also worth adding a laundry cleanser to remove any lingering bacteria and viruses, even on a cool wash cycle.

Beach towels can get stained by suncream which can be difficult to remove but try applying washing-up liquid to the stain before washing as above.

Picnic blankets

Picnic blankets can be washed easily in the machine using a cool, delicate wash cycle and a detergent suitable for delicates and wool. Always shake them thoroughly before putting into the machine to remove any loose dirt like grass, mud and sand. Allow the blankets to dry naturally and do not use the tumble dryer as this could cause shrinking.

Picnic blankets can become stained by grass and suncream which can be removed by pre-soaking in cool water. Apply washing-up liquid to remove suncream stains and a non-biological detergent to remove grass stains before washing as above.

Wetsuits

If you and your family love surfing, diving or swimming in the sea, then you probably own a wetsuit that can become quite smelly and dirty with seawater, salt, sand and suncream.

Wetsuits should be rinsed thoroughly in cool water as soon as possible after using them to remove as much of the seawater and sand as possible. They can then be washed in the machine on a cool, gentle wash cycle. You can purchase detergents specially made for washing wetsuits and prolonging the life of the fabric, but if you do not have one, then use one that is mild and non-biological. It's best to turn a wetsuit inside out before washing and always allow it to dry naturally. It is important that wetsuits are fully dried before packing away as they will become damp and smelly which won't be particularly pleasant next time you want to wear them.

Sleeping bags

We love camping and have always been camping with our families since we were children. I have so many happy memories of camping trips when I was growing up and although I love being at home, being outdoors having an adventure in nature is also one of my favourite things to do.

Sleeping bags should be washed at least once a season depending on how frequently you go camping. If you regularly use your sleeping bag, then it might be worth investing in a sleeping bag liner so that you can simply remove the liner and wash that more regularly rather than having to wash the whole thing.

Before washing your sleeping bag, check the care instructions as this will indicate whether it should be hand washed or if it is suitable for the washing machine.

Machine washing sleeping bags:

1. Unzip the sleeping bag so that it is fully open and can be washed thoroughly.

2. Use a delicate, cool wash cycle and a mild detergent. Do not use fabric conditioner.

3. Add a couple of tennis balls to the drum as this will stop the filling from clumping together.

4. Add an extra rinse cycle to ensure that all the detergent has been dissolved.

5. Remove the sleeping bag from the machine and roll it up to squeeze out the excess water. Do this over the bath or outdoors so that the water doesn't go everywhere.

Hand washing sleeping bags:

1. Fill a bath with cold water and a mild detergent.

2. Lay the sleeping bag down in the bath and ensure that it is fully submerged in the water.

3. Drain the soapy water and rinse with fresh cold water to remove all of the detergent.

4. Roll up the sleeping bag to squeeze out the excess water but be sure not to twist or wring it as this will damage the filling.

Drying sleeping bags:

You can either dry your sleeping bags naturally or in the tumble dryer. Keeping the sleeping bag unzipped and open, hang it to dry outdoors or lay it out on a towel to dry in a well-ventilated room. If using a tumble dryer, use a low heat and add a couple of tennis balls to stop the filling from clumping up.

Outdoor cushions

Outdoor cushions should be washed once a year but how you do this depends on whether the covers can be removed or not.

Cushions with removable covers:

1. Remove the cushion covers and put into the washing machine.

2. Use a cool wash with a mild detergent on a gentle wash cycle.

3. Allow to dry fully.

Cushions with non-removable covers:

Washing cushions with non-removable covers requires a little more effort, but I use the same method I use to clean my sofa indoors which I find works really effectively.

1. Add a non-biological detergent to a bucket or washing-up bowl of warm water and mix to create lots of foamy bubbles.

2. Using a soft brush or sponge, gently wipe the cushions using the foam. Be sure not to soak the cushions as this may leave watermarks and make the inner filling damp, causing mould.

3. Wipe using a clean, soft, damp microfibre cloth.

4. Use a dry towel to soak up any excess moisture and allow to dry fully before storing away for next year.

So, as you can tell from this chapter, there are endless seasonal tasks to complete but I always love a change in the seasons as moving from one to another is a gentle reminder that nothing lasts for ever and that we should treasure the memories we make as we travel through each one. I like to think that each season represents a new opportunity to go on adventures and make the most of the changes in temperature, whether it be snuggling up in a cosy blanket by the fire in the winter after a chilly walk with the dogs or a swim at the beach on a hot summer's day. Each of the items we wash is woven into these memories so I think having them fresh and clean helps to make them even more enjoyable.

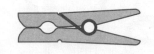

Laundry room: any
change left in pockets
will be considered a tip.

10

Babies' and children's laundry

We don't have children yet, but I'm sure many of you reading this already do, so you'll no doubt have much more experience than me when it comes to washing your little ones' clothing and bedding! However, after chatting a lot with friends, family and followers who have children, I've learned so many useful tips when it comes to children's laundry and hopefully this chapter will help simplify this type of laundry for you, whether you are a first-time parent, grandparent or helping out with a family member or friend's little ones. Thank you to all the wonderful parents who contributed their tips and advice to help me write this chapter for you.

Babies' sense of smell starts to develop in the third trimester so they will begin to recognise their mother's smell and other scents even while still in the womb. This is why newborn babies are more likely to settle with their birth mums as it gives them a sense of comfort. As they grow older, they develop the ability to distinguish between different smells. Strong fragrances can be overwhelming for babies, so it's important to be mindful of this when washing their clothing and bedding.

Babies' and children's skin is particularly sensitive, so when washing fabrics that will touch their skin extra care should be taken. Use non-biological detergents as these do not contain enzymes that could potentially irritate delicate skin. Liquids, gels or capsules are less harsh on fabrics than powders. Using a gentle fabric conditioner keeps clothing and bedding soft against their delicate skin and helps maintain the fibres, especially since it is likely that baby clothes will be washed a lot. Ideally it is best to stick to one detergent and fabric conditioner rather than switching as this could cause skin irritation. Unless items are heavily soiled, for most wash loads a cool 30°C temperature is sufficient. This will ensure the fabrics last longer and will save you energy at the same time.

Make your laundry life easier as a parent by purchasing fabrics that are practical and easy to wash. Cotton is ideal as it is soft against babies' skin and breathable, so it stops them getting too hot and is easy to wash. Cotton is also very durable so it can be washed multiple times, even on hotter temperatures if required. Nobody really has time to be hand washing at the best of times and definitely not as a parent, so avoid delicate fabrics as washing these will be more time consuming. Sometimes it is best when possible to invest a little more in buying quality cotton items that will last longer and you can even hand them down to family and friends, making them more sustainable.

Having lots of cotton muslin cloths is so helpful for a variety of uses including wiping up spills, acting as an emergency nappy change mat and creating shade, and they can be washed really easily multiple times. Cotton bibs are also a must-have as you can use them to protect baby clothes so when they dribble or are sick it is easy to whip off the bib and replace it rather than having to keep changing their clothing several times a day.

Laundry bags are ideal for washing baby laundry in particular as most items are so tiny – popping items like socks in them stops them getting lost.

Babies and children inevitably get dirty and have accidents so this section will give advice about disinfecting and washing their clothes and bedding to remove stains quickly and easily.

Removing stains

When baby clothes are soiled they should be washed separately to avoid contamination. Rather than using a hot wash which is expensive and can damage fabrics you can add a laundry cleanser or sanitiser to the wash. This is poured into the fabric softener section of the washing machine drawer and will kill bacteria and viruses in the wash, even on a cool cycle, so it is ideal for disinfecting clothes that have sick or poop on them. Dry the items as soon as the machine cycle finishes as damp clothes can be a breeding ground for germs. Ideally dry clothes outdoors as the sunshine acts as a natural stain remover and sanitiser.

For some additional information on removing specific types of stains, look no further!

Poop stains

1. Firstly, rinse the item with water to remove any soiling.

2. Pre-treat the stain with a liquid detergent and leave to soak for a few minutes.

3. Wash as normal using a detergent and laundry cleanser on a cool wash, or use a hot wash.

4. For fabric nappies it is best not to use fabric softener as this will reduce their absorbency.

5. Dry naturally, ideally in the sunshine which is a natural sanitiser and stain remover.

6. One of my dearest friends made a very valid point to romind all parents that on some occasions the inevitable poo-nami is not worth tackling and that sometimes you just have to admit defeat and put the soiled item in the bin!

Sick or vomit

If your child has been sick, then the easiest way to effectively remove the germs is to disinfect the fabrics using a laundry cleanser. If you do not have a laundry cleanser, then a hot wash (60°C+) will be required to break down any bacteria and viruses.

Food stains

1. Soak in cool water for a few hours or overnight, depending on the type and colour of the food. A dark or bright food stain like beetroot will need more time to soak than a lighter-coloured stain.

2. Rub laundry liquid onto the stain and leave for a few minutes before washing in the machine as normal.

Milk and formula stains

1. Blot with a damp cloth as soon as possible as these can be particularly stubborn if left to dry.

2. Soak for half an hour in warm water.

3. Rub liquid detergent onto the stain and leave for a few minutes before washing in the machine as normal.

Washing baby toys

Many soft baby toys can be machine washed, just pop them in a pillowcase or a laundry bag. There is no need to wash daily as it is good for babies to be exposed to a certain amount of everyday dirt and germs. If, however, there is a sickness bug in your household, then it is definitely worth washing them daily to avoid the spread of bacteria and viruses. Add a laundry cleanser to a wash with baby toys along with a non-bio detergent.

Our senses can be very soothing and also nostalgic, not only for us but for our families. The softness of a fabric when cuddling a child and the scent that is released when you touch a fabric can be very comforting. In my family we have always called it the 'family smell' – a scent that is unique to each and every family, reminding us of home and the happy memories we were fortunate enough to have growing up. Therefore, despite the mountains of laundry that babies and children create, try to find joy in the ritual of washing their clothes, treasuring the act of caring for your family and helping to create memories that they will subconsciously make positive associations with growing up. No matter how fast your laundry pile seems to grow, your children will be growing even faster so treasure making memories with them and don't put too much pressure on yourself. Remember that the laundry can always wait until tomorrow.

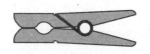

Laundry: for same day service, do it yourself.

11

Laundry for your pets

More of us than ever before now have pets – they are part of our families. We have two Italian greyhounds, Luther and Enzo, who may be small dogs but have a huge place in our hearts. When I met my partner Gavin over ten years ago he came as a package with Mittens, his half-Siamese cat, who we both loved dearly but sadly passed away a couple of years ago. Both Gavin and I have grown up with pets in our homes and to me, animals really make a house a home.

As any fellow pet parent will know, animals can make cleaning a challenge with the smells and stains they produce, not to mention the hair and mucky paw prints. If you worry about your house smelling like your pets, rather than trying to cover up any lingering odours, the best method is to regularly wash all of the fabrics that they come into contact with. Looking after our furry friends' laundry is essential in order to keep their bedding, blankets, collars, toys and even their coats and jumpers smelling fresh, clean and free from bacteria and allergens.

Animals have an extremely sensitive sense of smell and so when doing their laundry it is important not to use heavily fragranced products. We may love the scent but for our furry friends it can make them uncomfortable and they could have an allergic reaction so it is always best to opt for fragrance-free detergents. For pet laundry loads I also always replace scented fabric conditioner with white vinegar and a laundry cleanser (my dogs don't mind the smell of vinegar but using it in the machine dilutes it anyway so that when the laundry comes out, the scent has been neutralised). Adding half a cup of white vinegar in the fabric conditioner section of your washing machine drawer will act as a softener, neutralising any odours and also loosening any pet hairs at the same time. A laundry cleanser will then kill any bacteria lurking in the fibres of the fabrics.

Pet bedding

The easiest way to wash pet beds and blankets is in the washing machine. Firstly, vacuum them to remove the loose pet hairs before putting in the machine with a detergent and white vinegar. I also add a laundry cleanser which means that I can wash the items on a cool wash and still remove any bacteria. For any stains, pre-treat them by applying a liquid or gel detergent directly to the stain before putting it in the wash.

Pet beds and blankets should be washed weekly to help eliminate dirt, odours, bacteria and allergens. We have multiple dog beds to rotate between washes and find this really helpful because if your dogs are like Luther and Enzo who sleep for the majority of the day, then they will not be happy if they have to wait for their bed to dry after it has been washed.

You can also buy pet laundry bags to protect items in the washing machine and prevent any damage to zips or buttons.

If you have a particularly hairy pet, this can clog up the washing machine, causing damage, so I use the Vamoosh Pet Hair Remover which is the world's first pet hair remover for washing machines. It works by breaking down the hair in the machine using active oxygen, so removing it from your fabrics and stopping it getting trapped in your appliance at the same time.

Collars and harnesses

Collars and harnesses should be washed regularly to keep them smelling fresh and clean and to remove any dirt, mud and bacteria. How frequently you need to wash them will depend on your pet – how often they wear the collar and how muddy they like to get! I wash Luther and Enzo's harnesses and dog collars whenever they have a bath which for a short-haired breed of dog tends to be once a month depending on the time of year. If your pet goes to the groomer's, then after that would be the ideal time to wash collars and harnesses.

Fabric collars and harnesses

Fabric collars and harnesses should be hand washed by soaking in mild dog shampoo and hot water for 10–20 minutes. After soaking, gently scrub to remove any loose dirt. If there are still any stains on the items, then apply the shampoo directly to the stain and scrub using a toothbrush. Rinse thoroughly and then leave to dry naturally. It is also possible to wash fabric collars and harnesses in the machine by popping them in a laundry bag on a hand wash setting. As it always seems a waste just washing the dog collars and harnesses I fill up the machine with a blanket or dog bed which also helps to stop it making so much noise as it rattles around in the drum. It is worth bearing in mind that you will need to remove the bag containing the collars before giving the blankets and beds a spin or they will end up being sopping wet after just a hand wash cycle.

Leather collars

Leather collars should never be submerged in water. Instead, use a damp cloth to wipe the collar and a toothbrush to gently remove any dirt.

The worst occasion that I have had to wash Luther's collar was when he first discovered fox poop! I noticed him rubbing his neck on the grass looking like he was having the time of his life and then it clicked what he had found! I am sure that any fellow dog parents will agree that it is the worst-smelling odour that seems to linger for ever more and so cleaning their collar is key to getting rid of the foul smell. When this happened I asked my Instagram followers if they had any tips and they said to use tomato ketchup to get rid of fox poop although I never actually got around to testing it out. The collar was one of Luther's leather ones so I couldn't just throw it in the washing machine as this would have damaged it, so instead I soaked a microfibre cloth in hot water and laundry detergent. I then used the cloth to wipe the collar and a toothbrush to gently scrub, which seemed to do the trick.

Having spare collars and harnesses is useful so that you can rotate between them when the others are being washed and dried.

Pet coats and clothing

Luther and Enzo are a skinny short-haired breed so are very sensitive to the cold weather and refuse to go outside unless they are wrapped up warm. They have an array of jumpers and coats to keep them cosy and dry on their walks and they even have pyjamas to wear indoors when it's really cold! I wash these items using a delicate cool wash cycle along with a detergent, white vinegar and a laundry cleanser. This refreshes them so that they smell clean, are free from germs, and feel snuggly soft too. As the items are quite small and usually made by hand I use the delicate wash and pop them in a pet laundry bag to protect them and stop them getting damaged in the machine. I never use fabric conditioner on these items as they usually have a strong fragrance and can also damage the fibres on the fleecy jumpers or waterproof coats.

Pet toys

Luther and Enzo have lots of soft toys as they are sighthounds so love their fluffy foxes, hedgehogs and squirrels. Enzo always picks one up to give you as a gift whenever he sees you which is really cute, but they also love to play tug of war with them and usually rip them apart. It is important to wash pet toys regularly as they love to play with them in their mouths which can carry a lot of bacteria. Pet laundry bags are great for washing their soft toys in the washing machine with a detergent, white vinegar and a laundry cleanser to keep them smelling fresh and germ-free.

LAURA'S LITTLE LAUNDRY TIPS

Regularly wash your pet's beds and blankets. We love to snuggle up with the dogs and having plenty of blankets is an ideal way to protect your sofa. Pet beds and blankets can be the most common source of bad odours, so regularly washing them is an easy way to keep your home fresh. Pour white vinegar into your washing machine with a detergent to eliminate smells and give the beds and blankets a good shake and reshape when washed to keep them fluffy and cosy for your fur babies.

Laundry for your pets

Scent is extremely important to the wellbeing of our pets and they prefer either their own natural scent or our scent. Luther and Enzo love a freshly washed cosy bed, but the first thing they will always do is roll around in it to mark it with their own scent. They also frequently like to put their noses into the laundry basket and then proceed to run around the house carrying a pair of my dirty knickers or Gavin's dirty socks and this is because pets love the scent of their owners. Now clearly we can't have dirty laundry around the house just to keep our pets happy, but we can keep everything fresh and cleaned with their sensitive noses in mind by not using heavily fragranced products for their laundry.

Here are some tips for looking after your pet laundry:

- Regularly wash your pet's beds, blankets, collars, harnesses, clothing and toys to keep them clean as well as bacteria- and allergen-free – it will help keep your home smelling fresh.
- Replace fabric conditioner with white vinegar to keep pet laundry soft and fluffy while also loosening pet hairs from the fabrics and neutralising any odours.
- Pet laundry bags are great for washing fabric collars and harness, soft toys, coats and jumpers in the machine to avoid them being damaged.
- Have a spare set of collars, harnesses, blankets and beds so that you can rotate between them while the other set are being washed and dried.

✦ Use the patented Vamoosh Pet Hair Remover to break down pet hairs in your washing machine to keep the machine clean and running efficiently.

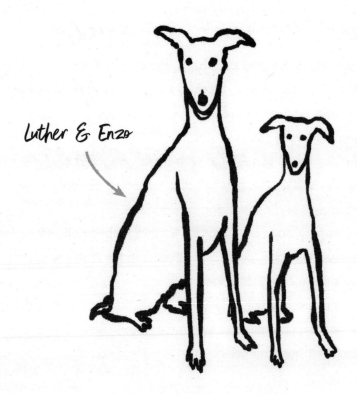

Luther & Enzo

Based on the amount of laundry in this place, there are people living here I have never met.

12

Laundry on the go

Travelling, whether it be for business or pleasure, can have its challenges when it comes to laundry. Often one of the most stressful things about coming back home from a relaxing holiday is the mountain of washing that has to be done when you return. When I was growing up, my family often went camping in France and I always remember my mum doing a couple of wash loads using the campsite facilities while we were on holiday. I used to think that was strange but now I can totally understand why she would do this!

Doing a little laundry while you are away on a trip is useful because it means you don't have to pack as many clothes in your suitcase and the post-holiday washing won't be such a daunting task when you return home. So, depending on what accommodation you are staying in, here are a few ways you can live your best laundry life on the go!

LAURA'S LITTLE LAUNDRY TIPS

When travelling, so that you don't have to buy laundry products which may be difficult to find in small quantities, pack liquid detergent and fabric conditioner in the travel bottles usually used for shampoo, conditioner and shower gel. Store in either a washbag or a ziplock just in case they leak. With a little bottle of liquid detergent you can not only wash your clothes while travelling but you can use it to pre-treat and remove stains on the go too.

If you are staying in a hotel, then they usually offer a laundry service, but it can be very expensive as they often charge per item so it is only really worthwhile if you have just one or two items that require a machine wash. A laundrette is also an option in many countries. Many road service stations now also offer a self-service washing machine, which is really convenient, particularly if you are camping.

If staying in self-catered accommodation, such as a campsite or an Airbnb, most of them will have a washing machine. When searching for accommodation before travelling you can usually filter to those with a washing machine if you know you'll probably want to use one. I find it so useful to have access to a washing machine if we are staying in a cottage or a villa or if we are camping as it really does help to keep on top of the laundry while we are away – even just doing one wash load really helps. If you are not sure how to use the washing machine in your accommodation, then you can always search for the appliance user instructions online as they are easily accessible in any language.

If you don't have access to a washing machine, then hand washing when travelling is a great option as it is cost effective and, in reality, most items don't get that dirty, they just need a little refresh. Use the sink in your hotel room or accommodation to gently wash items using a liquid detergent and then fabric conditioner. If you haven't packed or don't have access to laundry products, then soap or shampoo are an ideal alternative for hand washing. You can then use the shower to thoroughly rinse everything off before drying by wrapping in a towel to remove excess water and then hanging. Do not wring items as this can cause them to lose their shape.

There are also many gadgets that are available to help you do your laundry on the go including portable washing machines and the new electronic portable textile refreshers that use plasma technology to remove odours and bacteria from your clothes. Portable washing machines always seem like too much faff to me, but the portable textile refresher is fantastic for travel as it is so lightweight. However, it is currently quite expensive.

LAURA'S LITTLE LAUNDRY TIPS

I love to pop a couple of tumble dryer sheets in our suitcases, so that they smell lovely and fresh. I also always pack a carrier bag to put our dirty laundry in so that it is separate from the clean clothes. This makes it much easier to sort the laundry when you get home.

Drying can also be a challenge when travelling, so try to pack clothing that is easy to dry like synthetic fabrics, rather than cotton or denim which take much longer. If you're camping, then it is worth taking a clothes line or airer so that even if you don't do any laundry, you at least have somewhere to dry your towels and swimwear. Most self-catered accommodation with a washing machine should provide a line or airer but it is definitely worth contacting your host beforehand to double check.

When it comes to ironing, as you already know I rarely iron at home so it is even more unlikely that I will be ironing when travelling! But I do like to pack a crease releaser as I find these really useful for removing wrinkles in clothes and freshening them up at the same time. If you need to iron but don't have access to an iron when travelling, then a garment steamer is a great solution as they are relatively small and lightweight to pack.

Laundry on the go doesn't have to be complicated. Let's face it, nobody wants to be spending their holiday washing their clothes, but it can be really useful, particularly if you are travelling for a long period of time, and will definitely help minimise the dread of the post-holiday laundry stress.

Laundry rules: if it's not in the basket, it's not getting washed!

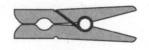

PART 3

Not
technically
laundry

(but still important!)

13

Drying

Thoroughly drying your clothes before storing them away is as important a part of the laundry process as the actual wash itself. I love to dry my laundry outdoors on the washing line on a warm sunny day as, not only does it dry so much faster, but it really is a lovely feeling to see your clothes and sheets gently blowing in the breeze. As soon as the sun comes out, I try to get as much washed as possible so that it can dry quickly. Unfortunately, here in the UK, warm, sunny days are few and far between, so the majority of my laundry has to be dried either in the tumble dryer or indoors on an airer. I used to use my tumble dryer all the time in the cooler months, but I am now being more conscious of the energy that I am using as the tumble dryer is quite thirsty when it comes to electricity and since energy prices have skyrocketed, the best option is to dry naturally.

Whether using your tumble dryer or drying your laundry naturally, there are a few things that you can do to speed up the process and, if you you're not a fan of ironing, also help reduce the number of creases. Here are the must-know basics for drying your clothes and other household items well:

- ✦ The drying process all starts in the washing machine, so avoid overfilling the drum as this can leave clothes damp and more creased.
- ✦ If using a tumble dryer, adding an extra spin cycle in the washing machine will help to reduce moisture.
- ✦ But if drying naturally, then it is better to use a slower spin cycle or your fabrics are likely to get more creased.
- ✦ Always remove items from the washing machine as soon as the cycle finishes as leaving them sitting in the drum for too long will cause creasing and a musty smell.
- ✦ Give items a good shake as soon as you remove them from the machine to help reshape them and start the circulation of air around the fabric.

Drying naturally

When drying your laundry naturally (either outdoors on a dry day or indoors when it's raining) it is always best to spread clothes out on the washing line or airer so that the air can circulate properly. Hang items about an inch apart and turn them after a couple of hours so that they dry fully. Invest in good-quality pegs to hang your washing on the line as I find that cheap ones will just perish, especially as they will be outdoors most of the time. As I mention

Drying

above, when you remove laundry from the machine, shake out each item individually with a sharp flick before hanging on the washing line as this works wonders to remove the creases.

Alongside good pegs, invest in a washing line that has plenty of space for the amount of laundry you need to dry in your household. Most lines state how many metres of space they offer so that is a good guide to help you choose the best one for you. Even in a small garden you can use a retractable washing line so it doesn't take up a lot of space. You can even get heated airers now which are ideal if you have a cold house and struggle with drying laundry indoors.

There are so many benefits to drying your laundry outdoors and, even if it isn't a warm, sunny day, providing it is not raining your clothes will still dry naturally (it will just take a little longer). Even on a cloudy day the sun's powerful rays act as a natural sanitiser, removing odours and enhancing the freshness of fabrics. The sunshine lightens stains and brightens whites. Your clothes will last longer by allowing them to dry naturally as there will be less damage to fabrics compared to using the tumbler dryer. It is quicker and safer to dry your clothes outdoors than drying indoors as there is more air circulating.

I like to look at the weather forecast and plan a laundry day when it is going to be good weather so I can get everything through the wash and out on the line to make the most of the sunshine. If your machine allows, you can even wash the first load on a timer so that it is ready to go out on the line first thing in the morning.

Laura's little self-care tips

Switch hanging your washing out from a dreaded chore to a ritual you enjoy. I find it so soothing to hang my clothes outdoors on the washing line with the sunshine on my face and a breeze giving me fresh air while moving my body in the morning. With our lives always being so busy, taking ten minutes to hang up the laundry can be a time for mindfulness to focus purely on pegging the items on the line and watching them gently blow in the breeze. Treat yourself to some cute pegs so you can focus on matching up the colours and take a second to observe the space around you, tune out from any stresses or worries you may have and think about what you're looking forward to in the day ahead.

When it's raining outside, like it tends to do very frequently here in the UK, drying indoors is your best option. Pop the airer up in a room with good air circulation, ideally with a window. Avoid bedrooms if you can as the dampness in the air can be bad for your health. You shouldn't use radiators to dry your laundry as this increases the dampness in the air, which can encourage mould spores to thrive, causing health risks and increase your energy bills as your radiators cannot do the job of heating your home efficiently if they are covered with wet clothes.

LAURA'S LITTLE LAUNDRY TIPS

A few years ago, we invested in a dehumidifier and we've found it really does help to dry our laundry indoors, although it is not cheap to run. We bought it when we lived in our first home, which was an old property that was quite cold and could be pretty damp in the winter so we found it hard to dry our washing properly indoors. We put the dehumidifier in the room with the laundry hanging on the airer, closed the windows and door and it really did help to speed up the drying process and stop our home feeling so damp and smelling musty.

I find that using fabric conditioner in a wash can also help to minimise that musty smell of damp laundry and keep your clothes smelling fresher for longer, whether they are dried naturally or in a tumble dryer.

Tumble drying

Tumble dryers are among the most energy-intensive devices in the home and it is no surprise that many of us are becoming more mindful of when we use them. However, if they're something you'd like to invest in, here's a handy guide to the three main types of tumble dryer:

Vented dryers

Vented tumble dryers have a pipe so that the moist air can be expelled. It needs to be positioned near a window or a wall with an extractor pipe. This type of tumble dryer tends to be the least efficient and most expensive to run.

Condenser dryers

Condenser tumble dryers are more efficient and so tend to be more affordable to run than vented dryers. Condenser dryers lift the moisture from your wet fabrics, collecting it in a container. The water is then either pumped out if your machine is plumbed in or you have to manually empty the container. We have a condenser dryer that is plumbed in and it does work effectively (although I am definitely noticing that with energy prices increasing it is becoming more expensive to run!).

Heat pump dryers

Heat pump dryers tend to be more expensive than other types of dryer, but are more energy efficient. They reheat and recirculate the air inside the drum therefore using less energy.

How much difference does energy rating make?

Here is an example of the difference in cost to run an energy-efficient dryer compared to one that is not as efficient. If you are thinking about getting a tumble dryer, then this is a useful guide to help understand the actual cost of running one. I've used 34p as my price per unit of energy in these calculations (see page 46).

Heat pump dryer A+++ rated
1.66 kwh (full load) x 34p = 56p per cycle
*Annual usage – 2 times per week = **£58.24 per year***
Annual usage – every day 365 days per year =
£204.44 per year

Vented dryer C rated
4.25 kwh (full load) x 34p = £1.44 per cycle
*Annual usage – 2 times per week = **£149.76 per year***
Annual usage – every day 365 days per year =
£525.60 per year

These calculations show that the A+++-rated heat pump dryer uses significantly less energy (kwh) and therefore costs less per cycle compared to the C-rated vented dryer. The annual cost difference is also significant, so I don't know about you but seeing these figures definitely makes me think more consciously about reducing the amount of times I use my tumble dryer.

Tumble drying top tips

If you have a dryer, no matter what its energy rating, there are some ways that you can make using it more effective and energy efficient at the same time.

- As mentioned before, add an extra spin cycle to the end of your wash to remove as much moisture as possible from the wash load before using the dryer.
- Shake your items before placing them into the dryer.
- To avoid unnecessary damage, turn garments inside out and fasten zips to stop them getting broken or snagging other items.
- Dry similar fabrics together using a suitable heat programme designed specifically for that fabric rather than a timer. The heat programmes use sensors to detect whether or not the fabrics are dry, which is more efficient than a timer that may last longer than required, wasting energy.
- Ensure the filters are clean and lint-free, and try to get into the habit of emptying them after every load. Although this might sound excessive, they can get clogged up very quickly and keeping them clear keeps your machine

running as efficiently as possible, reducing energy consumption and also avoiding fire risk.

✦ Use dryer balls to help the heat circulate between the fabrics efficiently.

✦ Position your dryer in a well-ventilated room, ideally one that is warm and dry. If your dryer is in a cold room like a garage, it will have to work harder, using more energy.

✦ Don't overload or underload your drum. Drying just a small amount of items is a waste of energy and overloading the machine is inefficient and can cause damage.

✦ Do not add damp items in the middle of a cycle as the drier clothes will absorb the moisture meaning the cycle will take longer to complete. It is more efficient to complete multiple loads immediately after each other as the heat will be maintained in the machine.

✦ Remove items from the tumble dryer as soon as the cycle finishes and shake individually before folding or hanging as this will stop them creasing.

When not to use your tumble dryer

When using your tumble dryer it is always important to check the garment care label. You can find all of the drying symbols on page 65. I always think, if in doubt, then leave it out and dry naturally. The heat in the tumble dryer can damage some fabrics and cause them to become misshapen or shrink, particularly items containing elastic or glue. These are the items you should not tumble dry:

- Wool
- Leather or faux leather
- Fur or faux fur
- Sequined or beaded items
- Silk
- Hosiery
- Suede
- Slippers
- Swimwear
- Bras
- Trainers

Not following the correct process to dry an item can cause damage or shrinkage or allow it to become misshapen. Hanging or folding things in your cupboards when they are still damp can cause them to smell musty, become creased and encourage mould to grow. If you are going to iron items straight after drying, then take them off the line or out of the tumble dryer when they are still slightly damp to make them easier to iron.

Let's get ready to
tumble!

14

Ironing

I must admit, I am not a fan of ironing and avoid it as much as I can. When we have guests over, I will always iron the bedding as I think it is important for the bed to look as inviting and cosy as possible for a relaxing stay. However, I don't often iron our own bedding as, although it looks beautiful when the sheets are crisp and wrinkle-free, in reality, I just simply don't have the time to do it!

But it's true that there are many benefits to ironing. For example, the heat removes bacteria, dust mites and bad odours, and it can also soften fabrics, making them look and feel really fresh.

In terms of day-to-day clothes it would make my life easier if I just ironed everything as soon as it was freshly washed and dried, which is what my mum has always done. I remember when we were younger, every evening after teatime without fail my mum would set up her ironing board and press all of the items that had been drying that day. At the time I never used to think anything of it as it was just her routine, but now, looking back, I am in awe of how hardworking she was, working full time with three young children and still managing to keep up with the housework. When I finally asked her about it, she said that she carefully positioned her ironing board so she could not only watch the television while she was ironing but she could also watch what was going on down the street! At that time, we used to live at the end of a cul-de-sac so she could see everything that was going on in the road from her ironing spot.

I think that my mum's secret to managing everything in the home was doing little and often, so by doing a little daily ironing session she didn't have a dreaded weekly ironing pile to tackle and she could do her bit for the neighbourhood watch at the same time!

I tend to just iron as and when I need a particular item of clothing for that day. I certainly don't iron underwear or socks! I think, as with any routine, you need to do what works for you and your household, so I am well aware that if I had a family of five, I would need to do things slightly differently. There are a few things that I do to make my life easier and they also help to motivate me to get the ironing done:

Top tips for easy ironing

- Put on some music, a podcast or the TV. I find this helps make the time pass faster. Having another focus somehow makes me forget about the pile of ironing in front of me!

- Invest in a quality steam generator iron (for more information on irons, see below) and I promise you that this will make your life so much easier. For years I always bought cheap irons that broke every few months and it wasn't until I started using a steam generator iron that my ironing game changed for the better. A quality iron should just glide through any creases with minimal effort. It might cost a little more initially, but it should last you for years to come which will save you money in the long-term, not having to replace it every few months like I used to have to do.

- Invest in a quality ironing board too, that has an adjustable height and a cover that reflects the heat, which also helps to make ironing more efficient.

- Make sure that your ironing board is adjusted to the correct height so that you are comfortable. You don't want to be bending or putting any unnecessary strain on your back as this will cause you discomfort, preventing you from wanting to iron anything.

✦ Do what you can to minimise excess creasing in fabrics in the first place. Using a fabric softener helps to reduce creasing in the wash, then as soon as your washing machine cycle finishes remove items from the machine and give them a good shake before letting gravity work its magic if hanging to dry naturally or using the tumble dryer.

✦ If using your tumble dryer, use dryer sheets as they reduce static and creases in the machine (and smell amazing too). It is also good to use tumble dryer balls as they help to circulate the fabrics and stop them from tangling up into a big mess which makes them really wrinkly.

✦ Iron your garments straight out of the tumble dryer when the fabric is still warm. This will prevent any creases setting into the garments when they come out of the dryer and cool down.

✦ Sort your freshly washed laundry into fabric types so that you don't have to keep changing the heat setting on your iron. Start with the items that only require a low heat setting like nylons, gradually working your way up to items like cottons that require a hotter setting.

✦ Remove deep creases by spritzing directly with a little water and ironing over the crease.

✦ Lay items along the length of the ironing board and use long, straight strokes to remove the creases. By zigzagging the iron all over the place this could add even more creases, so it is always best to stick to a long, straight motion to save you time.

✦ Reduce the sheen that you can sometimes get when the temperature is too hot when ironing a manmade material by always turning synthetic fabrics inside out before you iron them.

✦ Turn trouser pockets inside out before ironing to make it easier to get smooth results.

✦ Spritz a crease releaser onto the fabric before ironing. Crease releasers smell divine and make ironing even easier. I also use a crease releaser on our bedding as even though I don't iron it, it helps to remove the wrinkles so it doesn't look a complete crumpled mess!

LAURA'S LITTLE LAUNDRY TIPS

If your ironing board cover is not heat reflective, then why not try the tin foil trick? Lay tin foil shiny side up underneath your ironing board cover. This will make ironing easier as the heat will be reflected, applying it to the fabric from both directions at the same time.

Different types of iron

There are lots of different types of iron to suit every budget. Here's an introduction to the main varieties which are readily available:

Basic iron

A basic iron is relatively inexpensive to buy; it consists of a simple metal plate and a dial to set the temperature. As a basic iron does not have a water tank you will need a water spray bottle and starch spray to remove creases fully. Take care when using a basic iron as it can burn through fabrics.

LAURA'S LITTLE LAUNDRY TIPS

To remove scorch marks from fabrics if the iron was a little too hot, simply wipe using a clean cloth dipped in white vinegar then rinse with cold water.

Steam iron

Steam irons are the most widely available type of iron. They have a small tank to hold water that releases steam when you apply the iron to the fabric.

Steam generator iron

Steam generator irons have a separate water tank that releases more steam at a higher pressure than a normal steam iron. They are great for bedding and larger laundry loads as it is much faster and more efficient as you only have to iron one side of the fabric because the pressure of the steam removes creases from both the front and back at the same time. I have a steam generator iron and it is absolutely fantastic. They may be initially quite expensive but really do make ironing so much easier. The only disadvantage is that steam generator irons do tend to be bigger and bulkier, taking up more space.

Vertical steam iron

A vertical steam iron has a water tank to generate steam and then a handheld attachment which allows you to steam the garment vertically. The creases in the fabric are removed with no pressing required and no contact to the fabric so they are great for delicate garments. When I worked in retail, as stylists we would regularly use a vertical steam iron as it was easy to remove creases from the clothes on the hanger or on the mannequins.

Handheld garment steamer

A handheld garment steamer is small, lightweight and ideal for travel. It has a small water tank that generates steam to remove creases from garments without having to press them or contact the fabric. I find my garment steamer really useful for removing creases from bulky items that are not easy to iron like coats and curtains.

Trouser press

The only time I ever see a trouser press is when I stay in a hotel room. They give a professional finish to trousers, removing wrinkles and giving a sharp, smart crease so that you don't have to iron them.

Things to consider when buying an iron

When buying an iron there are a few different things to consider, including the various functions of the product, but ultimately it is worth thinking about your needs and how you intend to use it. So, for myself, as someone who avoids ironing, I have my steam generator iron for bedding and general ironing because even though it was an expensive appliance it really does make ironing so much easier and I don't mind that it is quite bulky as I just have it permanently on the worktop in my laundry room so I can use it whenever I need it. The other thing I love about my steam generator iron is that it identifies the optimum temperature for each garment, so I literally do not even have to think about burning anything. Even if I was to leave the iron placed down on the ironing board or on an item of clothing, it would not burn because it has a sensor that adjusts automatically. It is definitely ideal if you are prone to accidents! I then have my garment steamer for travel and particularly delicate items. Some of the features to consider when purchasing an iron are:

Water tank capacity
Depending on how much ironing you do, a larger water tank will mean you don't have to keep filling up the tank.

Anti-scale functions
If you live in a hard water area like we do, then this is a must as limescale can very easily damage your iron.

Cord length

These can vary depending on the iron so worth considering how long you need the cord to be so that you can easily position your iron and ironing board set-up in a convenient spot.

Auto switch-off

This is a great safety function to avoid any accidents if you forget to turn off the iron.

Ironing certain items can be particularly difficult and the most common questions I get asked are how to iron bedding, fitted sheets and shirts. So, I thought it would be helpful to share the tips I find useful for ironing these items.

How to iron duvet covers, non-fitted sheets and pillowcases

To make ironing the bedding easier, I always follow some simple steps for the washing. First, I fasten the buttons as this not only prevents the sheets from tangling up but it also stops the pillowcases and fitted sheet from getting stuck inside the duvet cover, not getting washed properly and everything coming out of the machine in a creased muddle. Remove your bedding from the machine as soon as it finishes the wash cycle, as this will prevent further wrinkles. Then dry your bedding either naturally outdoors on the washing line to let gravity help remove the creases or in the tumble dryer, throwing in a couple of tumble dryer balls to help the heat circulate and adding a dryer sheet to help reduce creasing.

Now, on to the ironing:

1. Before you begin, make sure you're ironing your bedding while it is still very slightly damp (either out of the tumble dryer or from the washing line). This will make the ironing so much easier.

2. Set up the ironing board next to your dining table so that you can lay the sheets across it, or you could pop a clean towel

underneath the ironing board so that the freshly washed bedding does not drag along the floor.

3. Lay the sheet flat on the ironing board then iron in long, straight strokes. I also spritz the fabric with a crease releaser to help make it even easier (and it smells lovely, too!).

4. I iron, then fold and repeat until I have a neat rectangle ready to dress the bed.

5. To iron the pillowcases, I lay them flat on the ironing board and iron right up to the edges to make them really crisp. I then fold and iron again to make a little square. For really stubborn creases you can put the inside of the pillowcase over the end of the ironing board so you are only ironing one layer of fabric.

How to iron fitted sheets

If ironing bedding wasn't tricky enough, then I think ironing a fitted sheet is even more fiddly! While they're a lot easier for making a bed, they're hard to iron well but hopefully with the below steps, you'll have it mastered in no time.

1. Attach the elasticated corners of the sheet to the edges of the ironing board so that it is as smooth as possible.

2. Iron the two corners and then the centre of the sheet.

3. Fold the sheet, matching the corners.

4. Tuck the elasticasted corners of the sheet into each other to fold the sheet and keep it together.

How to iron shirts

Shirts are a timeless staple item in every wardrobe, but they are also one of the trickiest items to iron. I have a few cotton and linen shirts that I wear as layering pieces and they can be quite fiddly to iron, but this is the easiest method I find that helps to give a crisp, crease-free result:

1. Check the care label to select the correct temperature setting for ironing your shirt.

2. Spritz the shirt with a starch spray or crease releaser and then leave for a minute before ironing.

3. Spritz any stubborn deep creases with water and then iron.

4. Start by ironing the outside of the collar. Lay the collar flat and press outwards from the neck to the edge of the collar.

5. Next, iron the cuffs. Open the cuffs up, and lay the underside flat on the ironing board. Iron outwards from the bottom of the arm to the edge of the cuff using the tip of the iron to get around the seams. Flip the cuff over and iron on the outside, avoiding the buttons as you don't want to melt them.

6. Move on to the sleeves. Lay the sleeve flat on the ironing board with the underside of the arm closest to you. Iron outwards from the seam to the edge and depending on whether you want a crisp crease or not, iron either all the way to the edge or just before it. Flip and repeat on the other side.

7. Now, on to the body. Lay one half flat and iron on the reverse of the shirt, then flip the shirt over and use the tip of the iron to get in between the buttons.

8. Finish by ironing the shoulders. Lay the shoulder flat and smooth out the fabric before carefully ironing to the edges.

9. Hang the shirt immediately to avoid creasing.

How to iron delicate items

Some fabrics may not be suitable for ironing, particularly delicates or those with embellishments or printed logos. Always check the fabric care label before ironing items and avoid ironing on the areas of items that might be damaged with heat.

Creases can be removed from delicate items with care either by using a handheld steamer so that no pressing is required or by using a crease releaser fabric spray. However, if you do not have either of these, another method that I picked up from my mum is to iron as normal but add a tea towel or sheet in between the iron and the delicate item to press it without applying the heat directly to it.

Ironing may not be everyone's favourite task, but hopefully these tips will help you to make it less of a chore and keep all of your fabrics crease-free and looking smart. Make your life easier by trying to minimise creases when washing and drying your fabrics. Invest in a decent iron that is suitable for your needs and try to crack on with the ironing when it is still slightly damp to avoid deep creases.

Laura's little self-care tips

If you are like me and not a fan of ironing, then it can be difficult to get motivated to start to make your way through that huge pile of freshly washed clothes. For a task like this that I usually really struggle with I try to shift my mindset and rather than focusing on the ironing, I use it as a time to get into my own zone. I tend to put on some music or a podcast and find that by focusing on listening to that I drift off and forget I am even ironing (much like my mum did watching TV and what our neighbours were up to!).

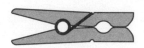

The most memorable
days usually end with
the dirtiest clothes.

A final note

So that brings us to the end of *Live, Laugh, Laundry*! While reading this book, unfortunately you won't have reduced your never-ending laundry pile, but hopefully it will have inspired you to change the way you approach washing your clothes and given you a sense of confidence and calm.

I wrote this book because I wanted to share my passion for doing the laundry as part of my self-care rituals. We all lead such busy lives, rarely making time for ourselves along the way, and I hope that I might have inspired you to make doing your laundry part of your self-care routine, too.

I feel like doing the laundry has become overcomplicated, so I hope that reading this has simplified it for you and will help you find a routine that works for you. Now you are equipped with strategies for removing stains with ease, knowledge of the best gadgets to invest in and how to give your washing machine some much needed TLC, and you can even be smug knowing about what goes in each section of the washing machine drawer!

Hopefully the energy-saving tips I have shared will encourage you to make tweaks to your laundry habits for the better, reducing your bills at the same time so you can treat yourself to something for you instead – maybe even some new divine-smelling laundry products.

I hope that reading this might also make you think differently about doing your laundry and showing yourself compassion, using the time you spend doing your laundry for practising mindfulness and rather than scrolling on your phone or worrying about everyday dilemmas, just focusing on the task in hand, letting your thoughts and feelings, stresses and problems drift away for a few moments.

Always remember not to put too much pressure on yourself and don't beat yourself up if you don't seem to be getting anywhere closer to the bottom of the laundry basket. One thing is for sure, there will *always* be laundry, but we are not here for ever and nor are our families, so the most important thing is to be happy and spend time with them making memories. Be comfortable with accepting that on some days the laundry can just wait.

Nurturing your laundry routine will help you to build resilience and give you a sense of control so that you can tackle the mountains of washing even on those days when your motivation levels are low. And, if all else fails, then just think of our ancestors many years ago taking their dirty clothes down to the river to wash them (thank goodness we don't have to do that nowadays!). But we can still make doing the laundry a sociable affair like they did by sharing our favourite products, tips and tricks.

A final note

I love to help others and I hope that by opening up about my struggles even as a laundry obsessive, this book will give you some reassurance that you are not alone. We are all just trying our best to get through each day the best way we can, so finding joy in the little moments we might normally be too busy to appreciate can only be a good thing, right?

Self-care for your laundry and, most importantly, self-care for you.

Lots of love,

Laura x

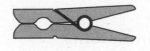

All you need is love . . .
and somebody to put
away the laundry.

The laundry products
I can't live without

In case it's useful, these are the laundry products that will *always* have a place next to my washing machine. They're all readily available in supermarkets or online.

All-in-one pods

These come in so many different scents to try and they are really convenient to use. You literally just throw them in the drum of your washing machine before filling it with your clothes and they dissolve in the wash. My favourites are the Bold, Ariel and Fairy ones. I use Bold if I want a strong scent, Ariel if I want to remove stains and Fairy for my bedding and towels.

Lenor fabric conditioner

This is the one when it comes to fabric conditioner in my opinion as the fragrances are absolutely divine and you can smell them on your clothes for ages. If you have followed me for a while, then you will know that I have always loved Lenor products. I love that you can buy all of them in the matching scents so you can have a whole collection of laundry products in your favourite scent. My favourite has to be Exotic Bloom but I love that Lenor regularly bring out new fragrances so I like to switch it up every now and then and try them for a bit of variety. For my American readers I think Lenor is the same as Downy in the US so I would love to know what scents you have and what your favourites are.

Lenor in-wash scent boosters

I absolutely love the scents of these little beads and, as I said, I use them all around my home as I just love the fragrance so much. My favourite scent is Exotic Bloom for my clothes but I also like to use the Fairy ones for my bedding and towels.

Lenor tumble dryer sheets

Even though I am trying to reduce the amount I use my tumble dryer, I still always have a pack of dryer sheets in my laundry cupboard as they are really handy to use all around your home to keep it smelling fresh. My favourite scents are Sparkling Bloom and Yellow Poppy but I wish they would make them in my favourite Exotic Bloom as I would definitely buy them!

DP soda crystals

These are a must-have for every laundry and cleaning cupboard and I always get asked where to buy them. They are available in most supermarkets or online and are only £1 so I always stock up on a few bags and I know my mum does too!

Cillit Bang White Vinegar with Eucalyptus

This is my favourite white vinegar as it has eucalyptus oil in it so doesn't smell as much like a chip shop as other vinegars.

Astonish Protect + Care Antibacterial Laundry Cleanser

This laundry cleanser claims to kill 99.9 per cent of bacteria and viruses including coronavirus and it comes in a Peony and Magnolia scent. I usually pick up a bottle when I am shopping in Home Bargains.

Dr Beckmann Re-usable Colour Collector

This is such a great product for throwing in mixed washes so that the colours don't run and the brilliant thing is that you can reuse it for up to 30 wash loads.

Vamoosh Pet Hair Dissolver

A must-have for pet parents, this patented formula is a really quick and easy solution for washing pet bedding and blankets, dissolving the hair to leave your washing machine clean and not clogged with pet hair. I always stock up on Vamoosh when I am shopping in B&M.

Astonish Oxy Active Plus Super Concentrated Fabric Stain Remover Powder

This is my favourite oxi powder as it can be used for both colours and whites, plus it is non-bio so it is great if you have sensitive skin. I always stock up on the huge 2kg tubs as they are the best value and I use this to keep my whites lovely and bright.

Ace for Whites Stain-Remover Spray

This is my favourite stain-remover spray as not only can it be used on your laundry but also to remove stains on white surfaces around your home, making it really versatile. I usually spritz some of this onto our white socks and leave for a few minutes before putting them in the machine and it brings them up like new.

You just hope that wherever all the socks go, they're happy. That's all that matters.

Thank you

Firstly, thank you to you for reading this book. I still can't believe that I have written my very first book and that you have a copy of it. I have always loved writing and it makes me so happy that you wanted to read it. I really hope you have picked up some useful tips to use and share, plus discovered a little bit more about me along the way. Grab this book whenever you need to make your laundry life easier; think of it as your little laundry encyclopaedia that can look cute next to your washing machine but, more importantly, let it be a sign to take more time for yourself and not feel guilty for it.

To my amazing followers, I absolutely would not have been given the opportunity to write this book without you and I will never forget that. I used to think that I was boring or strange for loving spending time in my home so much, but you gave me the confidence in myself that I am enough just by being me. Maybe one day I will be able to put into words just how much your support has lifted me during difficult times and in all honesty it's actually you who motivate me to clean my home and get my laundry done! Thank you for all the love you show me daily and, whether you are a new follower or you have been with me for a while, I hope we can continue to enjoy sharing our passion for a clean, cosy home for many years to come.

To my partner Gavin, you always give me the confidence to aim high, be brave and never look back. You cheer me on and keep me going when I feel like giving up. I love you very much and am excited for our future together.

To my Mum and Dad, I feel so incredibly fortunate to have you as my parents, I owe everything to you for all that you have done for our family to make us happy. James, Jessica and I grew up in a home so full of love and kindness with happy childhood memories that we will cherish forever, thanks to you both.

To my wonderful family and friends, thank you for all your love, loyalty, messages, voice notes and encouragement in all that I do. My circle is small and special, and I wouldn't have it any other way. You all know who you are and I truly treasure our friendship.

To my incredible Spotlight Team for believing in me and wholeheartedly backing my dreams. Alan, Ange and Heather not only are you the best team, but it feels like we have always been friends and I am eternally grateful for all your hard work and encouragement.

To my fabulous Ebury, Penguin Random House team for giving me an opportunity that I have always dreamed of. Thank you for your belief in me and your hard work and help in bringing my vision to life.

And finally, to my extremely talented editor Ru Merritt. Thank you for giving me my writing wings and helping me to fly.

All my love,
Laura x

About the author

Laura Mountford, aka @lauracleanaholic, shares her cleaning and laundry motivation, tips and tricks, favourite products and where to buy them on social media. Laura knows from first-hand experience that taking care of a home can be overwhelming but using products she loves and knows work well (and smell divine) motivates her to clean. Most of all, she finds that cleaning helps her to relax – it is an essential part of her self-care routine. Laura's belief is that everyone can care for themselves and care for their home at the same time.

Laundry notes

Live Laugh Laundry